WINNING THE PAPER WARS

MANAGE YOUR WAY TO GOOD WRITING

WINNING THE PAPER WARS
MANAGE YOUR WAY TO GOOD WRITING

Don M. Ricks

DOW JONES-IRWIN
Homewood, Illinois 60430

Sponsoring editor: *Jim Childs*
Project editor: *Karen Smith*
Production manager: *Faith Andre*
Jacket design: *Michael S. Finkelman*
Compositor: *BookMasters, Inc.*
Typeface: *11/13 Century Schoolbook*
Printer: *The Book Press, Inc.*

Library of Congress Cataloging-in-Publication Data

Ricks, Don M.
  Winning the paper wars : manage your way to good writing / Don M. Ricks.
    p.   cm.
  ISBN 1-55623-373-6
  1. Business writing.   I. Title.
HF5718.3.R53   1990
658.4'53—dc20   90-31400
                                                              CIP

Printed in the United States of America
1 2 3 4 5 6 7 8 9 0 BP 7 6 5 4 3 2 1 0

To Aunt Eleanor, with love

ACKNOWLEDGMENTS

Because this book is based on a professional lifetime, I've accumulated more debts than I can ever acknowledge. But I do want to thank Consultant, some of whose names are Jean Findlater, Janice Petty, Diane Bone, and Maria Van Brunt; also Marvin Lee, Linda Abercrombie, and Pat Holmes; and especially Barbara Lockwood—colleague, companion, and first mate of the *Maruba*.

Don M. Ricks

CONTENTS

INTRODUCTION

---

*Information has become
too important to success to allow it to go
wandering off in vague, directionless
memos and reports, ending up buried in
ignored piles of unreadable documents.*

I Try to Get Consultant to Understand

"Ha," I said.

"What are you going on about this time?" my friend Consultant asked.

"Here's an article in the paper that confirms what I was trying to make you understand yesterday. A Professor William Lutz has written a book about what he calls 'doublespeak' in business and government. For instance, he cites examples of companies that won't admit they are laying off workers. They claim they are having 'work force adjustments'—or people are being 'non-retained.' "

"And I suppose," Consultant said, "Professor Lutz is upset."

"He certainly is. The article quotes him directly: 'I have a real sense of outrage,' he says, 'that something as beautiful and powerful as language is being perverted.' So, Mr. Consultant, what do you think of that?"

"I think Professor Lutz sounds as though he's enjoying his indignation."

1

"No, no. . . . I mean what do you think about business people using words that way? What do you think of a company like Chrysler, when it lays off hundreds of workers, claiming it has 'initiated a career alternative enhancement program'? "

"With all respect to Lee Iacocca, I think it was a dumb thing for Chrysler's management to say. They are experienced executives who had to make some responsible and painful decisions in order to keep their Company healthy. They shouldn't have then explained their actions in words that make them sound foolish, or perhaps dishonest."

"Well!" I said. "I never thought I'd hear you. . . ."

"The whole problem of bad writing in organizations is much different—and much more serious—than eggheads like you and Professor Lutz know. A muddled, unreadable document is not a philosophical offense against the English language. It's a bad way to do business. In an age when accessible, usable information increasingly constitutes power and wealth, organizations that continue to block their communications with old-fashioned, self-protective writing practices will find themselves growing weaker and poorer."

"But. . . ."

"As I said, I have a project for you. I'm going to help you write a book that tells executives how to take control of written communications. We're going to show them how— finally—they can stop writing from being an unnecessary drain on energy and resources . . . how they can convert it into an efficient tool their organization uses in getting its work done. So I don't want you nattering at them about grammar and rhetoric and appeasing professional outrage. People have been listening to the English teachers too long already. You're going to talk business to them."

"Well, yes, I suppose I am, . . . but. . . ."

"You complain about the occasional muddy letter from your insurance company or the tax department. But suppose you had to come to work every morning knowing a *stack* of that kind of writing was waiting on your desk. Just imagine what it's like to be a mid- to senior-level manager trying to run a complex operation while having to depend, for information, on wordy, unfocused documents that are unpleasant to read and difficult to understand. Now more than ever, managers need help in changing the ways their organizations write. Information has become too important to success to allow it to go wandering off in vague, directionless memos and reports, ending up buried in ignored piles of unreadable documents.

"But certainly you can't believe business writers shouldn't be expected to. . . ."

Consultant ignored me. "But no one has yet offered business executives realistic advice on *how to get their people to actually start writing more readable documents.* Managers keep taking measures they think will encourage employees to write more lucid, functional prose . . . but nothing changes; people just keep on writing the same way they always have. So you are *not* going to scold executives. And you are *not* going to give them a lot of dull advice on good writing. Instead, you're going to tell them how—finally—to get people to start doing it."

"That's exactly what I was wondering about," I was able to say, finally. "Why does the problem seem so difficult? Why don't people in business and government just . . . just start writing more clearly?"

"Because of the Paper Wars."

"What?"

"The Paper Wars."

CHAPTER 1

CONSULTANT TELLS ME
ABOUT THE PAPER WARS

---

*Many executives think there's
something inappropriate, even
dangerous, about writing in direct and
explicit language. They don't know how
to give people permission to write well.*

Who's Fighting? Over What?

Consultant said that the Paper Wars are a conflict in business and government between people who want to get things done and people who want to be careful; between those who think the first job of the writer is communication and those who think it is protection and preservation. One side insists, "We must make ourselves understood"; the other side counters, "We don't dare."

"Those who prefer the established ways," Consultant said, "treat writing essentially as an act of self-defense. They favor limited disclosure, careful explanation, and strict adherence to whatever cautious practices have, thanks to precedence, been deemed 'acceptable.' "

He went on to tell me about Paper Wars combatants he'd met over the years. There were all those bosses who kept his consulting business solvent by sending their employees to his writing workshops—then insisted, when people returned to their desks, they continue to write exactly as they did before the training. He also talked about the frustrated managers who are still trying to solve the same business writing problems—with the same methods—that have bedeviled them for most of their careers. And about the tribulations of the engineer who always tried to avoid English in school but learned, when he graduated into the working world, that almost every project begins with a written proposal and ends with a written report. And about the frustrated department head whose memo just came back completely redrafted by her boss. And about her boss, an experienced, highly paid executive who spends much of her time working as other people's rewrite editor.

The rumblings of the Paper Wars can be heard in the staff room, where people complain of the frustrations felt by those who have to *write* as part of their work. They talk of management's vague directions, unreasonable or irrelevant criteria, compulsive editing, and their own wasted efforts as they spend 20 percent or more of their time performing a difficult and distasteful task, often unsuccessfully.

In the executive suite, on the other hand, Paper Wars veterans complain about the frustrations of having to *read* as part of their work: rambling, self-protective memos; unfocused letters written for carefully concealed reasons; long reports that give mountains of facts but little information; written instructions that are not clear even about the task to be done, let alone how to do it. Managers know every major decision they make is based upon a written report or proposal, and they are painfully aware they often cannot understand much of what the document says.

Yet when open warfare breaks out—when, for instance, the president declares he is "not going to read any more of this junk," or when senior managers realize that a key project is in danger of being smothered by bad paper—the actions that typically follow only add to the damage. Elaborate writing guidelines are drawn up; silly compromises are forced by those who insist on protecting favorite practices; a communications expert or a professor is called in to speak to those least responsible for the problem; and people are left with more to argue about and even fewer insights into what they are expected to accomplish when they write.

Management's Self-Inflicted Wound

"What you have to understand," Consultant said, "is that the Paper Wars are fueled by an uncertainty about whether or not people are *supposed* to write well. Many managers think there's something inappropriate, even dangerous, about writing in direct and explicit language. But at the same time, they are frustrated by having to read so many documents written in evasive, writer-protective circumlocutions. Because they have ambivalent feelings about writing themselves, they signal ambiguous expectations to their people.

"As a result, when they try to make things better, they often end up making them even worse. They don't know how to give people permission to write well. Sit down. I'll tell you one of my favorite war stories."

The Boss Writes a Memo

"Here's a memo our boss wrote," one of the workshop participants said. "What do you think of it?"

A hush fell over the room. Consultant looked around warily, instincts alerted. Judging from their expectant expressions, everyone was familiar with the memo.

The long opening paragraph, an extended acknowledgment of the importance to the company of good communications, was clearly leading up to something the writer considered significant. Exactly what could only be guessed at.

The second paragraph, which began, "As you know, time is money," explained the details of a recent study on how much it costs an organization to write memos.

As the group watched, Consultant turned to the second page. It too led off with a long paragraph, one intended, apparently, to make people aware that the boss was a busy person; that he had to absorb a great deal of information, track many separate projects, and constantly make important decisions; and that long, rambling memos made his job unnecessarily difficult and frustrating.

"Therefore," the memo decreed well down on the second page, "all memos written by employees of this company will now be strictly limited to *one page* in length."

In passing the incident on to me, Consultant insisted, "The point you must stress is *not* just that the boss did something dumb in sending out a two-page memo declaring others were to write one-page memos. What you want to emphasize when you use the story is that the boss tried to bring about change by proclaiming other people were to perform a behavior he considered too risky to perform himself."

"Too risky?" I asked. "What's so risky about writing a one-page memo?"

"Think about it," he said impatiently. "We're not concerned that the memo was two pages long, but that it was one-and-a-half pages longer than necessary. What the boss perceived as too risky was the technique all writers must use in order to write succinctly—he should have made an early and explicit purpose statement. If he had said, in the opening paragraph, that he wanted to put a one-page limit on memos, his own memo would have ended well under one page. If he had been willing to make his point first, then explain it, he simply wouldn't have felt compelled to go on about all that other stuff nobody needed to hear anyway. And he would have modeled for his people the way he wanted them to write."

"So, why didn't he state his purpose in the first paragraph?"

"I already told you. He was afraid."

"Of what?"

"Of being perceived as unreasonable, or perhaps even incorrect. He felt he needed to build a big case first—before he told people what he had in mind—because he thought that otherwise he might not be taken seriously. And the result is not pleasant to think about."

"How do you mean?"

"As a result of trying to make sure he was taken seriously, he guaranteed he was *not* taken seriously. In fact, his memo became a department joke—something so funny it was worth sharing with outsiders. His employees were entertained, not impressed.

"As a reader, the boss knew exactly what he wanted other writers to do. But when he sat down to a blank sheet of paper, the writer within himself refused to do it. So his employees could ignore what he was trying to accomplish in writing the memo. After all, if the boss actually liked short memos, he would have written one himself. Moreover, all serious talk of streamlining memo writing subsequently became tabu in the department. No one, including the boss, dared raise the issue again, knowing that derisive chuckles were sure to follow.

"What you have to explain," Consultant said, "is that many managers are sending out some very confusing messages. They insist they want good writing, but they behave in ways that make people think they prefer bad writing . . . and will enforce it. Therefore you not only have to tell people how to *win* the Paper Wars; you have to persuade them to *stop doing things that assure they continue losing them.*"

Consultant Explains My Assignment

Consultant says that the Information Age caught the executive suite unprepared. Because of changes that have taken place in a few short years, more people now have to send and receive, understand and remember, more information than ever before. And they have to communicate more complex ideas—and communicate them more quickly, efficiently, and accurately—to a broader range of audiences than ever before. Modern technology has not diminished our dependence on written communications; it has increased that dependence. It is no secret, for instance, that the personal computer boom was almost smothered in its crib by unreadable user manuals.

But today the cold shadow of the past lies on written communications more than on any other organizational activity. The executive suite is trying to forge its way into the 21st century dragging behind the unsolved writing problems of the 20th century; and it is carting along its 19th-century nonsolutions as well.

Therefore, Consultant said, he would help me write a book for and about the people who run corporations and agencies, the ones who have to use written communications as a way of getting things done.

"You'll have to tell managers to smarten up," Consultant said. "You'll have to help them understand that the disease, bad writing, is much more painful than the cure. When they give up the notion that people *have to* write badly; that they *can't* write any differently; they'll discover that the victory—achieving competent, constructive written communications—is relatively easy."

He went on to talk about what my book would accomplish. He said it will tell managers how—after all these years of trying to battle the same writing problems with the same unsuccessful weapons—they can attack *the real problem, their own ambivalent attitudes and behaviors toward writing*. He said the book will make them aware how they inadvertently sponsor and perpetuate bad writing even while trying to get good writing.

Consultant said the book will also offer people ownership and control by demystifying writing, showing them it is a form of work that sensible adults can make intelligent and safe decisions about. "Executives need to know," he said, "that they do not have to become quasi-English teachers in order to get people to write well, . . . that as soon as they get in touch with blocked expertise already existing within themselves, their writing, and their organization's, will start improving immediately."

In short, he insisted, the book will be about how to *win* the Paper Wars. It will show executives how they can assure written communication becomes an effective tool for achieving corporate goals—rather than a continuing battle ground between frustrated readers and confused writers.

Now that I understand my assignment, I can explain all these things in good time. For now, let's listen in on another of Consultant's war stories.

The Leaky Offshore Drilling Manual

The assignment was typically vague. Senior Engineer, head of the Offshore Drilling Department in a multinational oil company, had asked Consultant to "take a look at" a manual and "suggest ways it might be improved."

The manual, which had been jointly written by a dozen engineers over the space of a year, was intended to assure that good procedures were followed if an emergency occurred during an offshore drilling operation. So the stakes were potentially high—blowouts and fires, dead and injured, front-page coverage of giant oil slicks. The manual was important to the engineering staff as well. They were proud of it, seeing it as an original contribution to safety in a new and dangerous field.

The people who were supposed to read and be guided by the manual were the drilling foremen (or "drillers"), the mud-spattered men who are responsible, in eight-hour shifts, for the operation of a multimillion dollar drilling rig and the work and welfare of its crew. Drillers learn their jobs, and earn their jobs, the hard way—on the rig deck. Many have a high school education or less.

Senior Engineer explained to Consultant that a copy of the manual would be located in the "dog house" (a small, shed-like structure where the crew eats and rests) of every offshore rig. He realized that the drillers were unlikely to read the entire manual. But he hoped that, during quiet times, they would "glance through" it, thereby becoming familiar with the information it contained. If an emergency developed, a driller was to consult the manual to determine how to react.

Some images began to form in Consultant's mind, pictures that apparently had not occurred to Senior Engineer. Consultant envisioned a driller entering a dog house to relax for a few minutes. The dog houses Consultant had seen were littered with reading materials, usually magazines featuring nude young women or paperbacks with western and science fiction themes. What would be likely to tempt a driller (assuming he was a reader at all) to forgo this more attractive fare in favor of poking around in the emergency procedures manual?

Then another scenario began to form, one in which a driller entered the dog house and reached for the manual. This one included flames glimpsed through dense smoke, the shock of explosions and the grind of collapsing steel. What would happen if an emergency did occur on a drilling rig? How would the manual be used by an emotionally overcharged person who needed to react promptly and precisely to one of humankind's newer and more complicated experiences, the technological disaster?

Filing these images away for future reference, Consultant turned to the manual, looked through it, and found it was a disaster itself. The information it contained was obviously important and carefully thought through, but the document itself was unreadable. The "look through" that Senior Engineer hoped for would last about twenty seconds, the time it took each driller to decide the manual was written by engineers for engineers, not for drillers. They would not understand many of the words used. The long, elaborately modified sentences would be difficult for them to track. Drillers would not know that, to find the most important information, they should search among the ends of paragraphs and the closings of sections, not at the beginnings.

The manual would have been useless in an emergency. The more elaborate parts read like answers to examination questions in an engineering course; others read like notes taken during the lectures. The manual was laden with discrete statements of fact, but sparse on interpretation and explanation. It was precisely organized, with each chapter, section, and paragraph carefully numbered and subnumbered just the way the textbooks say. But the very detail obscured the organizational pattern. The elaborate table of contents—which, according to Senior Engineer, was to guide drillers in finding the information they needed—would take several minutes to read.

In a subsequent meeting, the manual's audience-insensitive methods were staunchly defended by Senior Engineer.

CONSULTANT:

In the rush of an emergency, people think they don't have time to look up something in a table of contents or an index. Instead, they will thumb through a document looking for words that relate to the subject they want to know about. So I suggest that you replace the numeric system with prominent key word headings on each page.

SENIOR ENGINEER:

We worked for days developing that numbering system. I believe it's the heart of the manual.

CONSULTANT:

> On each page you have two numbers, the chapter number at the top and the page number at the bottom. The reader can't readily tell which is which. Why not just have your secretary reprogram the word processor to add the words "Chapter" and "Page" before each number?

SENIOR ENGINEER:

> There's no need. After the people on the rigs use the manual a few times, they'll figure out the difference.

(One often encounters, in such Paper Wars skirmishes, a stick-to-our-guns attitude, an apparent fear that giving ground on any single matter may endanger the whole position being defended.)

To Consultant the issue was clear. Senior Engineer and his staff were trying to do an important, difficult writing job, and they needed professional help. The present document was, at best, just a rough content base that had to be totally rethought and rewritten before the manual would work for the drillers on their windy platforms in the sea. The only question was whether the client was prepared to make the necessary investment.

To Senior Engineer the issue was entirely different— but equally clear. The manual just needed a little polishing up, a task that he and his staff were perfectly capable of performing. But they were busy with other, more important, projects, so he was thinking of contracting out the work. He figured the job would take only a few days, and, since it did not even require an engineer, should be worth about fifteen dollars an hour. He had been looking for an English teacher to check the manual for spelling and grammar. Instead, someone had sent him this so-called consultant who seemed determined to tear up the whole book and start over.

The outcome, Consultant now assumes, was that the company eventually produced and distributed the manual, at considerable expense, in something close to its original form. He also assumes that the occasional copy can still be found, battered but unread, under the magazines and paperbacks in the dog houses of several offshore drilling rigs. Since the press has not named that company in any major disaster stories, it perhaps matters little who won or who lost, who was the hero and who the villain, in that minor skirmish in the Paper Wars. But the values they fought over would have been interesting, had they met to explain them.

CONSULTANT:

> Communicating is important. Your company has assigned the drillers a big and potentially disastrous job. It's your duty to help them by giving them guidance in a clear, accessible document that expresses ideas in language they understand, not in language you learned in engineering school. It's pointless to talk about how they *should* read the manual. You have to respond to the realities of how they *will* read the manual—or, given almost any excuse, *will not* read it.

SENIOR ENGINEER:

> You're proposing to rewrite a manual that contains our information, our expertise. Since you're not an engineer, you probably don't even understand most of it. If we let you change our ideas into different language, how can we be sure you won't change our meaning as well? The drillers are employees of this company. They are responsible for knowing where to find out how to handle emergencies. This manual gives them that information, and it's up to them to figure it out.

Perhaps Senior Engineer—at some level below awareness—did not even believe that written words can truly communicate, can actually direct and control the behavior of people like the drillers. Perhaps for him, having to participate in the writing of the emergency drilling procedures manual was simply one more episode in the struggle that had been going on since he was in school. It continued the conflict between himself and those who kept insisting that words are tools, not mysteries; that mastering their use is important; and that unless he kept writing he could not be Senior Engineer any more. Perhaps, therefore, his real objective was simply to get the job done, regardless of how well. He wanted to bring in an English teacher only to protect himself from those errors that others seemed to spot so readily. Otherwise, he simply wanted to see the manual bound, distributed, and behind him. Whatever his reasons, Senior Engineer sacrificed an innovative and important document, settling for a manual that he could explain and defend rather than one that would help the drillers cope in an emergency.

Senior Engineer had the satisfaction of winning the skirmish. It was an easy Paper Wars victory, of course, a simple demonstration of the decisive power of inertia. To exclude Consultant and his discomforting point of view, Senior Engineer had only to remain unconvinced that Consultant's services were needed. Those who do not get hired do not get heard.

Consultant was not blameless, however. Too certain of the obvious rightness of his own values, he neither recognized nor honored the values of Senior Engineer. Senior Engineer saw himself as a winner. With his help and direction a group of engineers had achieved a considerable feat, the creation of a lengthy written document. By discrediting that achievement, by treating the manual as a seriously flawed preliminary draft, Consultant created a win-lose situation, one he was sure to lose. Once egos clashed, the outcome was inevitable.

Had Senior Engineer been more receptive to ideas and values that challenged his own, or had Consultant been more skillful and patient in presenting them, a truly useful, standard-setting manual might have been written. The burned hulks of lost opportunities litter the battle grounds of the Paper Wars. People often wince at the bad documents that get written, but now and then one also hears a wistful sigh for the good ones that were prevented.

CHAPTER 2

THE ISSUE

Nobody likes to read BoG
(the Business or Government style).
People only want to write it.

What Kind of War Is This, Anyway?

My Job as your reporter on the Paper Wars would be much easier if I could use the old journalistic trick of simplifying the issue into a conflict between the good guys and the bad guys, with people like Consultant representing one side and Senior Engineer the other. But the Paper Wars are more complicated than that.

As Consultant admits, it's not always easy to decide who to sympathize with, whose side to line up on. Paper Wars victories are few, and often petty. Defeats are frequent and shared by all. It little matters, when bad communications cause a major client to defect to a competitor, that someone sounded the warning. The lucrative project that dies stillborn, strangled by bad paper; the big sale that never gets closed because the buyer cannot understand the proposal; the costly screwup caused by vaguely written instructions; such events can trigger blame and recrimination. But they can never earn vindication for anyone. Those who were right lose just as surely as those who were wrong.

In these Wars one can seldom be sure, in the midst of battle, even about what people are fighting over. The apparent objectives of either side, ambiguous to begin with, can change from day to day. At any given time who is defending, and what, and what the offense is trying to achieve, and why—all can be obscure. Allies change sides, perhaps so quietly that no one notices until the ambush.

Yet ultimately—whatever flag the combatants may claim they are rallying to—the Paper Wars are being waged over a single issue. They are a fight to assert the supremacy, in the written communications of each organization, of one of two forms of expression. One form we can call CleaR writing. The other we'll call BoG (for Business or Government) writing.

BoG versus CleaR

Here is a paragraph from a progress report written by a practitioner of BoG.

> As Appendix C indicates, certain discrepancies appear when our test results are compared with those of the other lab. Discussions have been initiated with our counterparts there and it is hoped that a definitive answer will be available in two weeks. Although the discrepancies appear to be minor, especially in comparison with the significant benefits offered by the project, it would seem advisable to delay a final recommendation until they have been resolved.

Here is the same paragraph, but written by a practitioner of BoG's opposite, CleaR.

> At this point the project looks very beneficial. Our final recommendation will be delayed for two weeks, however. We need time to sort out, with our counterparts at the other lab, some minor discrepancies between their test results and ours (see Appendix C).

Consultant once polled his associates, and they all agreed. They had never talked to anyone who likes to read BoG. People only want to write it.

What BoG Is

BoG, a form of writing that is endemic to business and government, is the result of the consistent use of certain writing practices that result in documents having four identifying characteristics:

1. Their purpose is ambiguous or even obscure.
2. They are difficult to read and understand.
3. They provide too little information, too much information, or irrelevant information; as well, the meaning and significance of the information they give is unclear.
4. Sometimes they do not feel right. Their tone is unnecessarily cold or defensive or offensive.

In other words, BoG is a complete system for bad writing. Its techniques can be taught, modeled, explained, and enforced. It comes complete with stylistic practices, conventional information patterns, and organizing strategies. It also includes a complete set of justifications, rationalizations, and defenses to counter the impertinent objections of those who try to claim that bad writing is not a good thing to do.

Bad writing is *not* a good thing to do, of course. To begin with, it costs too much. People can write CleaR documents more quickly and easily than they can write BoG documents. And CleaR documents require fewer drafts and less manager editing.

BoG is also counterproductive. It obscures rather than clarifies, angers rather than mollifies. The person who writes BoG in hopes of sounding informed and professional comes across as being confused and unable to communicate. The manual intended to simplify a job, if written in BoG, will make that job more difficult. When the recommendation report is badly written the time and effort that should be invested in making a good decision will be expended instead in puzzling out the case the writer was trying to make. A client is likely to buy a competitor's product if the purchasing committee is confused about what our proposal is offering to sell them. Projects have been screwed up in very expensive ways simply because the people doing the job could not understand the documents intended to help them.

Besides being self-defeating, bad writing also gives people too much to argue about. It is both the cause and the effect of the Paper Wars. Energies better invested in accomplishing real goals are diverted into squabbles and compromises, drafts and redrafts, stern pronouncements and petty subterfuges.

If the prevailing form of business or government writing, BoG, is such a bad thing, how then did one of the wonders of the 20th century, the modern, technological organization, come to be the source and citadel of so much of it? CleaR—the clean, easily read alternative to BoG that turns facts into purposeful, structured, accessible information—is no mystery. Some people in most organizations write it every day. Yet why do proponents of CleaR, especially now with the Information Age fully launched, still find themselves having to fight for its general adoption? Why do some managers continue to defend BoG, even while complaining of their organizations' written communications problems and stalwartly proclaiming their intentions to modernize and simplify its writing? To begin to understand these questions, we have to look at the origins of BoG.

Where BoG Came From

"How did the practice of writing BoG get started?" I asked.

"No one knows for sure," Consultant answered. "We can only speculate."

"Speculate for me."

Consultant said he believes obscure, complicated forms of writing similar to BoG had probably been around, in academic and legal documents, since the 19th century. But the current version did not become entrenched in business and government until the years immediately following World War II. That was when 20th-century technology collided head-on with the organizational structures, writing traditions, and linguistic assumptions of the 19th century. Within a relatively short time organizations became much larger and more complicated than ever before. They began to perform tasks no one had even imagined previously. Rather suddenly, a whole generation of scientists, managers, and administrators had to learn to function—and to communicate—within structures originally evolved as a way of organizing people to do labor-intensive, technologically simple work.

Men and women who, in other years, might not have written fifty letters or memos in a working lifetime had to write a dozen a week. Those whose writing experience consisted of a few school essays and lab reports became responsible for managing the writing of multivolume proposals for massive projects.

And no one knew how to proceed. People had to write far more than ever before, and for totally new reasons. Yet they had no relevant traditions, no precedents to follow. They had been intimidated by English teachers who taught them the purpose of writing was to write correctly. They had been miseducated by academics who had taught them the purpose of writing was to write profoundly—and at length. As well, they found themselves trying to communicate within a new organizational structure that soon taught them the purpose of writing might be to say little—as carefully as possible.

As new kinds of specialists were brought in to do new kinds of jobs, many of the comfortable verities that underlay the communications practices of the traditional organization began to break down. Confusion—with undertones of paranoia—was inevitable. People became less sure of where they fit, of how their functions were supposed to interact with the functions of others, and of how they individually were supposed to relate and communicate with others.

People had to adapt to radical changes in the implicit relationships not only between superiors and subordinates but between peers as well. The individual and departmental linkages within organizations multiplied in number and complexity as the new technologies became more varied and specialized. An elaborate spiderweb of new dependencies was spun, which became entangled with both the formal lines of authority laid out by the organizational chart and with the informal network of friendships and contacts that shapes much organizational behavior.

The introduction of computers provides the classic case study of the tensions that can be created by major technological innovation. Newly graduated programmer/analysts—people with little organizational experience, uncertain organizational status, and often the overconfidence and impatience of youth—became involved in very direct, precise, and disruptive ways in the day-to-day operations of established departments. Their clients were usually the organization's most senior managers, people of experience, maturity, and wisdom who nevertheless felt some resentment of, and vulnerability to, the intruders. Both groups, moreover, had their own jargon, their own mysteries, as well as a sense of commitment to the integrity of their own professions. Confusion of roles and ambiguities of status and function were inevitable. Some people had the necessary capabilities, others the necessary power, and no one was sure who was to direct whom, or how. Walking on eggs became habitual, and people grew sensitive to every potentiality for disagreement and ego damage.

As organizations became bigger and more complicated, the task of communications became bigger and more complicated too. Writing in particular began to take on a new importance and to use up increasing amounts of an organization's energies. Previously, when corporations and even government agencies were smaller and more localized, people had plenty of opportunities to talk with each other. Internal written communications were used primarily for record-keeping purposes. Moreover, they were limited largely to the higher levels of organizations, and they amounted to little more than what-to-do memos flowing downwards and what's-been-done reports flowing up. But as the modern organization evolved, almost everyone above the rank of craftsman had to start writing, and reading, as a regular part of their work. And writing increasingly became a means of getting others—who were often superiors or peers in different departments—to do things the writer needed to have done, and to do them in ways the writer wanted.

"You have to remember as well," Consultant reminded me, "not only do organizations operate much differently than they did 50 years ago, but many of the people who have to write as part of their work have complicated jobs that were not even invented 50 years ago. So there's a professional self-consciousness in much organizational writing, a sense that the writer must carefully justify everything he says. I remember, as an undergraduate in the 1950s, taking the introductory courses in a wide range of relatively 'new' academic subjects—economics, psychology, sociology, and journalism, for instance. In almost every course, the professor started off with a lecture arguing that the field of study deserved recognition as being either 'scientific' or 'professional.' If the professors felt their own status needed defending, it's little wonder their graduates left feeling the same uncertainties."

So two contradictory dynamics developed simultaneously. At precisely the time when organizations were expanding rapidly in size, diversity, and technological sophistication, their internal components were becoming increasingly isolated by specialization, tunnel-visioned professionalism, and ambiguities of role function and relationship. In short, when people most needed to start writing to each other in intelligent and helpful ways, they found they were not sure of what they were supposed to say or of how they were supposed to say it.

The people who were in charge, anxious to get on with exploiting the opportunities of heady new technologies, and distracted by the multitude of new problems posed by the modern organization, turned to the least appropriate models—academics and lawyers—and on their example invented and perpetuated the form of written expression Consultant has named BoG. Those who led the technological explosion are often people who, by both temperament and education, distrust what happens when ideas are committed to paper. Therefore, they readily embraced a kind of writing that seems, above all, to be careful.

Let's think about these creators, first sponsors, and most consistent—but by no means exclusive—defenders of entrenched bad writing in business and government, the *aliterate* executives.

CHAPTER 3

THE COMBATANTS

*The decision we have
to make is whether we want to be
people who produce reader effective—
or writer protective—documents.*

The Alits

People love to misunderstand when Consultant uses the expression, "aliterate executive." Depending on their Paper Wars allegiance, they want either to cheer or fight back. But *aliterate* does not mean *illiterate;* it does not even mean *nonliterate; aliterate* means simply *other than literate.* Consultant uses the word not only descriptively, but nonjudgmentally and entirely empathetically as well. Most aliterates in management positions are competent readers and writers; some are unusually skilled at both. They are as intelligent (or stupid), as creative (or unimaginative), as likeable (or offensive) as their more language sensitive colleagues. But aliterates are *different* from their literate colleagues, and understanding that difference is one key to understanding what is going on in the Paper Wars.

People have different kinds of minds: different ways of processing sensory information; different ways of formulating, storing, and expressing concepts. Without delving into the psychology involved, we can look at one primary dichotomy—between people who think *symbolically* and those who think *verbally.* Math versus English . . . the Sciences versus the Humanities . . . *alits* versus *lits.*

In other words, we're talking about capabilities, not disabilities. And we are concerned with the broad center, not the lightly populated extremes. Certainly we have heard of the poet who can not multiply and of the statistician who can not write a simple declarative sentence. But both belong to tiny minorities at the distant ends of the curve. Most of us fall much nearer the median. The alit sketches out ideas in diagrams, then searches for words to explain them. The lit, on the other hand, first writes the report, then designs diagrams to illustrate the text.

Obviously people who are more symbolic than verbal are most likely to succeed in those professions where symbolic thought and expression are required. Alits become mathematicians, engineers, systems analysts, and architects—and often senior executives in large technological organizations. The lits, who are more verbal than symbolic in their thinking, become lawyers, psychologists, writers, and teachers—sometimes English teachers.

Consultant insists that, in contrasting the roles of lits and alits in the Paper Wars, my purpose is to explain the differences between how each behaves and why, not to scold or expose anyone. Nor should I suggest that the Paper Wars are *between* lits and alits. Rather, they are *among* lits and alits. Consultant has known many alits who, having learned to listen to the right voices within themselves, are staunch defenders of CleaR. And he's known some lits, individuals skilled in the art of corporate politics, who speak as strongly in favor of BoG. People of either orientation can find themselves, in any particular skirmish, fighting in either camp.

Further, alits do not deserve to be cast as the bad guys in the Paper Wars. There are no villains in these organizational skirmishes, just people of differing points of view who are trying to do the best job they can with the resources they have.

On the other hand, Consultant says my job is not to praise his foes. When all other alternatives have been eliminated except open battle, he has usually found himself, perhaps shoulder-to-shoulder with some lits, charging the crumbled fortifications of rules and precedents behind which alits entrench themselves.

If I sometimes seem harsh in criticizing alit managers, I am simply venting Consultant's frustration at the exasperating number of times they have repulsed his efforts. The first step in any purposeful organizational change process is to "unfreeze" the thinking of those involved. But too often his consulting skills have not been adequate to thaw the barriers many alits have erected against what for them are the dangerous vagaries of the written language. When Consultant fails to help, or when he manages to help less than he might, he prefers to blame the client's intransigence rather than acknowledge his own lack of competence.

On the other hand, Consultant and I both understand the predicament of alits. Most never claimed to be anything other than what they are—mathematical, scientific, symbolic thinkers who quite happily would leave writing to those who are interested in such things. One of their goals in school was to survive English, and they hoped that all that talk about report writing was just an empty threat.

But life played them a dirty trick. When they finally escaped schools, teachers, and troublesome writing assignments, they were hired by organizations that immediately put them to work writing. As junior employees they found that, to the higher echelons of the corporate hierarchy, they were only a name on the FROM line of memos and reports. As they matured they often came to manage groups whose work was pointless unless reported in a written form usable by others. The people who never wanted to write anything, ever again, in effect became semiprofessional writers and editors.

It's little wonder, then, they turned for guidance to the part of their training that made the most sense—the Mighty Nevers. Forced by circumstances and the needs of their organization into the dangerous activity of putting words down on paper, they made the quite reasonable deduction that one should at least be sure to avoid those practices known to draw criticism. Whether one could ever write *well* was debatable. But certainly a person should try to write *safely*. He should learn what *not* to do and be assiduous in enforcing those negatives in his own and other's writing.

Alits could not be expected to recognize that the oft-cited rules have little to do with how readers interact with the written language. The old, dependable Mighty Nevers are but the inventions of others who were themselves trying to put down a few safe anchors in the sea of lit glibness. The English teacher, motivated by a mildly uncomfortable self-consciousness, ventures to suggest that writers "should use the first-person pronoun *I* as infrequently as possible." Years later an alit manager, sensing immediate relief for some of his own discomforts with writing, proclaims a Never: "Never use the word *I* in any document written on company letterhead."

Although some alit senior executives seem—from Consultant's point of view certainly—to be more unreasonable and less tractable than others, they are not to blame for the Paper Wars. They deeply believe in the rightness of their approach to writing and its values to their organization. (Nor are the younger employees to blame, despite the criticism often directed their way. Raised by the TV set, schooled in communications rather than English, and launched into the working world with marginal writing skills, they are usually the first casualties, the innocent bystanders, in the Paper Wars.)

The battle is not between the just and the unjust, nor between the informed and the ignorant, nor even between individuals who champion opposing points of view that are fully formed and consistent. The manager who today demands CleaR may tomorrow edit it out of a report written by a subordinate. Conversely, good writers in a company may defend, in the work of others, BoG writing practices they do not honor in their own documents. Most individual executives, at any given time, are as likely to be on one side of the fight as on the other. Often the only discernable difference between a nonpracticing lit and a practicing alit is a visible tightening of the jaw when a favorite Mighty Never is challenged.

The Birth of a Mighty Never

A Drama in Two (Very Short) Acts

Cast

Miss Rice, a third-grade teacher, twenty-two years old.
Charlie, a boy, nine.
Mr. Charles Hepner (Charlie forty-six years later), CEO of a large corporation.
Louis, a public relations consultant hired to help Mr. Hepner polish up a speech he has just written.

Act One

Scene. A classroom. Children's pictures on the wall, etc.

(Enter Charlie, late again.)

MISS RICE:

(Sternly.) The bell rang ten minutes ago, Charlie. Why are you late this time?

CHARLIE:

(Sullenly.) 'Cuz I missed the bus.

MISS RICE:

(Hoping only to cure Charlie of speaking in incomplete sentences.) Charlie, don't you know you're never supposed to begin a sentence with "because"?

Act Two

Scene. A plush business office, walnut paneling, etc. Mr. Hepner and Louis seated at a large desk, side-by-side.

LOUIS:

> (*Politely.*) Let's see what we can do with this paragraph, the one beginning, "It is unquestionable that certain negative manifestations will take place in the economy, and that these manifestations will be directly attributable to the recent changes in the tax laws."

MR. HEPNER:

> (*Defensively.*) What's wrong with that? It sounds okay to me.

LOUIS:

> (*Placatingly.*) There's nothing really wrong with it, Mr. Hepner. Let's just see if we can give it a little more punch . . . get to the point a little sooner.

MR. HEPNER:

> (*Sullenly.*) Well don't give it too much "punch." This speech is for a business conference, you know, not a revival meeting. It's supposed to be dignified.

LOUIS:

> (*Thoughtfully.*) Suppose we started with, "Because of recent changes in the tax laws. . . ."

MR. HEPNER:

> (*Triumphantly.*) Louis, don't you know that you're never supposed to begin a sentence with "because"?

Curtain

Stand Tall Alits

There is no shame, when the muster of alits is called, in stepping forward. Consultant and I do not use the term opprobriously and hope no one else does on our example. Symbolic thinkers are the creators of the modern, technological society and all its wonders and comforts. We lits, if you had left progress to us, would still be scratching our way through life with quill pens, by candlelight.

If you are an alit some parts of this book may not be comfortable to read. But please remember that you are the object, not the subject, of the book; you are the person it was written for, not about. After a professional lifetime of working with people like you, Consultant thinks he and I can help, and in ways that will be important to you.

Showing you how to make things better will be easy. The difficult task will be to help you recognize and stop doing certain actions that, however reasonable they may seem, have persisted in making things worse. If we sometimes are critical, remember that we are trying to bring into sharp focus truths that deeply affect your own success and that of your organization.

We also want to explain *you* to our fellow lits. We want them to know that your world works differently than theirs; that your ways of knowing are as valid as their ways of knowing; that your ways of thinking can be as creative as theirs; that you may have been balked and frustrated in ways they have not; and that you may have had to learn different means of coping than they have.

Finally, we want to invite you to a new understanding of us lits as well, and to a new partnership with us. Technical information is the most valued commodity of the Information Age. You own the raw materials; we know how to process them. Together we can flourish and prosper.

But first I am going to have to talk about the way you do some tasks Consultant says you are not very good at. And about how you came to be the inadvertent defenders of a false faith, the proponents and propagators of forms of communication that serve you and others badly.

The Lits

Consultant and I are, of course, lits. Again, terms need to be defined carefully. The words *lit* and *alit* acknowledge differences in psychological makeup, while *literate* and *illiterate* acknowledge differences in learned skills. A very large proportion of the world's population, being victims of educational deprivation, are stone-cold illiterates, even though tens of millions of them are lits by psychological bent.

Moreover, *lit* does not include the meaning *literary* (although few alits produce best-selling novels). When it comes to either reading or writing works of literature, lits, like other people, live along a continuum ranging from regularly to never.

Lits are simply those people in the population for whom words, especially in their written form, are an easy and natural way to transmit and receive information and ideas. Words are their friends, not their potential enemies.

School was often an affirming time for lits. A poem worked for them the way the algebraic equation worked for symbolic thinkers; it was the door to new and interesting perceptions. Even Physics could be figured out if one did enough digging in the textbook. And teachers always prefer to work with verbal pupils; the results of their instruction are mirrored back to them so much more readily. A lit with a little knowledge could knock out a high scoring essay the night before the deadline; a studious alit might have to work for days just to produce one that would pass.

On the job, alits sometimes find lits' ways with the language suspiciously cavalier. Having taken many examinations (often designed and graded by others like themselves), alits are sure that a one-to-one relationship exists between words and ideas. A certain combination of words earns full credit; one or two deletions or substitutions costs points. Yet lits freely switch words and sentences around, experimenting with alternative ways of expressing the same idea. They happily discard hard-learned technical terms, replacing them with simple words one hears every day—or worse yet, with similes and metaphors.

Lits are wasteful, too. When they write a report, their trash baskets are likely to fill up with discards from their experimentation. If an alit asks their advice on a document, he is likely to find a painfully constructed paragraph reduced to a single sentence that, the lit insists, "says everything the reader needs to know." Alits have to work too hard for their words; once they have some nailed down on the page, they prefer to keep them.

Lits are often among the walking wounded in the Paper Wars. Doomed to champion writing practices that seem dangerously innovative to those in power, they lose more battles than they win. Their most carefully planned attacks can be routed by a resurrected pronouncement uttered long ago by a sixth-grade teacher or an engineering professor. Entrenched alits, when passing final judgment, recognize no appeals against the Mighty Nevers, the ancient and holy words that will protect us all.

Despite their scars, lits seldom have much effect on the ways their organizations write. The alits who usually run things have found practicing lits to be more troublesome than useful, so they have cast them in supporting roles. Most lits tend to be concentrated in areas such as human resources and public relations, where they have little influence and almost no power.

Certainly many senior executives are themselves lits. But they are usually of the nonpracticing variety. However important their fluency may have been in their success, it was probably perceived as only an incidental competency as they climbed the ladder. ("By the way, he writes excellent reports, too.")

Many senior people have found that a sensitivity to language can be inconvenient. Everyone loses when a meeting gets sidetracked into a debate over a question of rhetoric. Having learned the ice is thin in certain spots, they long ago opted to skate on other ponds. Junior lits, delighted to discover behind closed doors a high-ranking ally in the battle for good communications, often find themselves unsupported when a showdown comes. Veterans of the Paper Wars know that victory can sometimes cost too much. An unforgiving opponent, defeated on a point of communication today, can torpedo a pet project next week.

I don't mean to make too much of lits. They are no better (or worse) than alits. They are no wiser or better informed, no more honest or trustworthy. They are simply more likely, when left to their own instincts, to turn out a clear, purposeful letter or report, and more likely to make decisions about written communications that respond effectively to the needs of readers.

As well, they probably win more arguments than alits (even while losing more battles). Alits themselves cite instances of their own inability to defend a sound idea from the attacks of a fluent lit who "can talk circles around me." Knowing exactly what they meant but unsure how to say it, alits have been victimized by glib lits (who have even been known, for the sheer joy they take in manipulating words, to say things they do not mean).

Yet lits do have a major and surprising handicap in the Paper Wars—they have a *shortage of words* that can be used in talking about good writing. The alits have a formidable arsenal—an accumulation of rationalizations, myths, supposedly inviolable rules and principles, as well as certain logical and linguistic argumentative strategies—to use in defending their basic position, that writing is dangerous and therefore must be done carefully and in certain prescribed ways. The schools have armed the proponents of BoG well, giving them long lists of all the words likely to be misused and of all the writing practices to be avoided because they are "incorrect" or (powerful word) "unacceptable."

Lits are more lightly armed. Academics, preoccupied with correcting bad writing, have given little concrete indication of what they think *good* writing is. Bad writing incites them to detailed annotations: "Unclear." "Ambiguous." "Faulty parallelism." "Dangling modifier." "Split infinitive." "What on earth do you mean?" "What point are you trying to make?" "Confusing." "Vague pronoun." "Comma splice." "Poor paragraph coherence." "Hasty and shoddy work." "D."

Good writing, on the other hand, stirs only an occasional subjective generalization: "Good Point." "Well developed paragraph." "An interesting and informative paper." But otherwise, when a lit looks for terminology to make a case for positive writing practices, the academic establishment offers only a collection of obvious bell ringers that working adults could pretty well figure out for themselves: "Say what you mean." "Be specific." "Keep your reader in mind." "Write purposefully." "Use no more words than necessary." (Consultant says he has never met, in over 30 years of teaching writing, anyone who perceived himself as using unnecessary words. If the writer didn't think he needed them, he wouldn't have written them down.)

Such exhortations are quite valuable; without them, those who lecture on good writing would be stuck for something to say. But they are not much use to a person sitting at his desk staring at a blank piece of paper. They cannot get him started on that report due tomorrow; and they cannot help him explain the complicated idea his boss told him to include—the one he is not sure either of them understands. And the general pronouncements of the academics are certainly not weapons that can be wielded in the Paper Wars. The person who has to argue for a revision on the grounds that "this way just seems to state the idea more directly" only confirms what her opponents have long suspected: Lits, even though they may not know what they're talking about, are willing to take unnecessary risks.

Later I will explain, in more depth, Consultant's assertion that many alits believe writing is dangerous. But first, let's have another of his war stories.

The Professor's Six Writing Styles

The contract, long in fruition, had developed into a prize. Under the enthusiastic sponsorship of a key Vice President,

Consultant and his associates had been conducting a series of report writing workshops. The results were coming in— company executives were saying they were starting to make better decisions, easier and more quickly, because they were receiving more useful reports.

Vice President was beaming; Consultant was proud; Consultant's bank manager was free to worry about other accounts.

Then one morning, when Consultant arrived to set up for that week's workshop, Vice President was waiting at the door of the training room, a stack of papers in hand.

"I've found a great article on business writing. I made copies of it so you can use it in the workshop."

The customer, they say, is always right. So Consultant— knowing he had to get his flip charts made up before people started filing into the room, and knowing, from the expression on VP's face, that he was more than pleased about his new contribution to the training project—started to search for a quick but not-too-dirty escape from his dilemma.

Consultant never incorporates other people's materials into his own workshops. The practice is, to begin with, distracting to the course participants. Integrating outside materials into a carefully planned learning process, and ironing out any real or imagined contradictions between the native and foreign points of view, are not only distracting but take time and energy. The intruding documents seldom justify the effort.

Yet that argument seemed, to Consultant, a bit subtle under the circumstances, as he and VP stood at the door of the training room with people passing in the hall and the clock ticking away.

He could also explain to the VP that those who photocopy other people's intellectual property without paying pre- agreed compensation violate their own country's copyright laws and the provisions of several international treaties. But calling a favorite client a thief did not seem a good way to start the day, either.

What Consultant was most reluctant to tell the Vice President was that he had recognized the article immediately, as he had read it recently and was appalled by what it said.

The article appeared (not that long ago, even now) in North America's most prestigious business journal. Its author, a professor of management communication with impressive academic credentials, was himself associated with the journal. Consultant knew then (and I myself know now) that one does not lightly dismiss the work of such an eminent personage.

But the article had left him dumbfounded.

It proposed that, in business writing, *six* different writing styles can be identified. It further proposed that, if one is to write competently, one must be able to write *all six*— and one must further be able to recognize which of the six is most appropriate to different purposes. (Even though, as the professor pointed out, he found it impossible himself to generalize about which style was best in what situations.)

Consultant knew what would happen to a person's present writing if he was told he had to learn to write six different styles. It would be similar to what would happen to a person's golf swing if the club pro told him he had to learn, on his backswing, to bring the club head to six different positions, depending on his club selection and the objectives of the shot. Incapacitation, that's what would result. The writer would be left staring numbly at the blank sheet of paper, just as the golfer would be fortunate even to make contact with the ball.

Consultant also knew what would happen in the training room if certain alits read an article confirming their assumption that writing is a complicated, dangerous activity which carries a high probability of making revealing mis-judgments. The professor proposed that, when writing in re-sponse to *negative* situations, a person should use the style that was, of the six, the most impersonal and inexplicit. As Consultant knew, many alits think having to write is, by def-inition, a negative situation; and they always favor the im-personal, indirect strategies of BoG. He believed people need assurance they can learn to write well, not an expert's ac-knowledgment they can never write safely.

Further, Consultant (himself once a "publishing" aca-demic) knew that such articles are seldom intended to be taken literally. The professor had indeed structured his arti-cle in a "how to do it" format. But he had probably never considered what might happen if someone, sitting at a real desk with a real writing job to do, actually tried to follow his advice. Academic articles are written as displays of erudi-tion, not work aids.

Faced with the risk of making his client feel like either a dupe or a copyright violator, Consultant chose the only real option available—cowardly compromise. Taking the stack of paper from the VP, he promised to "work the article into the course, if we have the time."

Fortunately, the Vice President never asked.

As Grown-Ups, We Get to Decide

One of the payoffs of surviving to adulthood is that we have broader opportunities to decide for ourselves what we're go-ing to be. The Professor's article on the six writing styles evokes, for example, the identity crisis of people like Con-sultant who offer themselves up as teachers to the organi-zation. Are they innovators or preservers? Do they teach people *better* ways of doing things, or do they simply teach them the ways management likes to have things done? Or, for that matter, do they teach the old ways of doing things, but invent new names for them? Organizational coffers sometimes open readily to those who offer the apparent excitement of new ideas without threatening the status quo.

The Professor, in opting to describe the six styles (including three forms of BoG) he discerned in business writing, and in opting to explain how each was to be properly used, chose to reassure those in power that nothing was essentially wrong with their system of writing; it just needed finer tuning.

Consultant has chosen to be the bearer of a message that, obviously, is not so comforting. Compared with the Professor's pat on the head, what he says to his clients is likely to feel more like a kick in the pants. But he has elected to become a worker for constructive change rather than a preserver of mediocrity.

So he has to break eggs. At his suggestion, this book accuses many key executives of behaving in ways that encourage and perpetuate bad writing, to considerable cost to themselves and those around them. Its explicit purpose is to stir up, disturb, and agitate in order to create a seedbed in which new and more productive writing behaviors can grow. Those who wish to solve—finally—the seemingly perpetual problems of corporate written communications must surrender many of the comforting verities that have sustained them to this point. They must also get involved in matters that until now they have happily left to others. In other words, they too have to decide what they are going *to be:* opponents or defenders of bad writing.

Each organization, each leader in business and government, each individual who has to write as part of his or her work, gets to make some choices, too, about how they are going to present themselves in the documents they produce. Both as individuals and organizations we can choose whether to speak in the lucid, confident voice of CleaR, or the hesitant circumlocutions of BoG.

The decision we have to make, then, is whether we want to be people who produce *reader effective—or writer protective*—documents. Unfortunately, no comfortable compromises are available; we can't do both. The writing practices that feel safest to the writer of BoG are the ones most frustrating to readers. And the CleaR practices that communicate openly, directly, and efficiently are the very ones most likely (initially at least) to feel risky to a writer who is used to hiding behind BoG.

But why does the choice seem so difficult? *What are people so afraid of, anyway?* Perhaps the time has come to hazard a peek at the Bogeymen.

CHAPTER 4

THE BOGEYMEN

We disguise our Bogeymen
behind careful rationalizations—
behind elaborate explanations of the
special constraints under which
business writers, especially in our
own organization, must write.

How the Bogeys Were Discovered

Asked to explain in one sentence the essential nature of BoG, Consultant once answered: "It creates the impression of having been written by people who are frightened." He says BoG is pervaded by a feeling that the writer, forced by circumstances to commit thoughts to paper, is irrevocably exposed to the possibility of censure in some form. The following memo, written by a practitioner of BoG, illustrates what he means.

> Your request for July vacation dates has been received and careful consideration has been given to same.
>
> As you know, the Gibson report is scheduled for completion on August 1st. In addition, two employees with more seniority than you have requested July dates as well. Therefore, we would be very short-handed if I approved the vacation dates that all three of you have requested.
>
> Please feel free to discuss this matter with me at your earliest convenience.

Here is the same memo, but written by a practitioner of CleaR.

> I'm sorry to say that I can't approve the July vacation dates you requested.

Two others with more seniority than you have asked to go then, so I'll need your help in finishing the Gibson report by the August 1st deadline.

Let's get together and look at other dates.

The writer of CleaR comes across as frank, decisive, and constructive. The writer of BoG—who, as both a person and a manager, is probably equally admirable—projects an image of being defensive, equivocal, and uncertain. Somehow he couldn't bring himself to actually say, on paper, that he was not approving the requested vacation dates, and the memo he wrote to close the matter seems in fact to invite the reader to press his case further. The elaborate, explanatory strategy of the memo suggests every sentence is intended to deflect an anticipated criticism.

Long ago Consultant concluded that there must be some sort of Bogeymen behind BoG.

> **bo·gey, bo·gy,** bo´ge, n. [W. *bwg, bwgan,* a hobgoblin, scarecrow, bug-bear] A hobgoblin; a fearsome specter; any object of dread. Also **bo·gey·man.**

Nothing else could account for the fact that grown men and women—skilled, educated people who are capable of managing complicated functions in corporations and agencies—often sound like scared rabbits on paper. But sorting out the various hobgoblins proved as challenging and frustrating as playing a new computer game. Every time Consultant learned to identify and neutralize one spook, a new one would attack from a different direction and in a different form.

Eventually, however, Consultant began to distinguish three generations of "fearsome specters": the Corporate Bogeys, the Profession Bogeys, and the School Bogeys. He also discovered the secret of identifying Bogeymen. Like the devil, who tries to hide his tail, the Bogeys have a trait that is a dead giveaway. Their name is always followed by the word *might*. "If I include something the VP already knows about, he might be offended." "If I tell my boss what I want right at the beginning, he might say just say no and not bother to read the rest of my memo." "You shouldn't say that in a report; somebody might think you're being too informal." "I can't put that in; someone might get mad at me!"

Let's start with a look at the youngest and least threatening generation, the Corporate Bogeys.

The Corporate Bogeys

Bogeys do not exist in the external world, of course. They are internal creatures born into the psyche of each of us, spawned by our emotional responses to specific experiences. Consultant calls the Corporate Bogeys the "youngest generation" because they are the most recently formed. They were born after we became adults and started working. All companies and agencies, and often individual departments within them, adhere to certain writing practices that they consider uniquely their own, the "way we always do it." They perceive one of their first tasks, when newcomers are brought in, is teaching them to comply with the writing behaviors that appease the local Bogeys.

Here is a story about one in action. It showed up hidden behind a favorite alias of Corporate Bogeys, *my boss*. Remember, you'll be able to recognize the Bogeyman in the story by the revealing word, *might*, following his name.

WORKSHOP PARTICIPANT:

What a neat technique. It would really improve our reports. Too bad we can't use it.

CONSULTANT:

You can't use it?

WORKSHOP PARTICIPANT:

No, my boss might not like it.

CONSULTANT:

(*Having over the years lost dozens of arguments with bosses he never met, and feeling the tickle of inspiration.*) It's not even 4:30 yet. You can probably catch your boss before he leaves.

Why don't you go show him your report and ask him what he thinks? We can talk about it tomorrow.

(*The next morning.*)

WORKSHOP PARTICIPANT:

My boss loves it! He says it would be the best thing we could do to improve our report writing. He's really sorry we can't use it.

CONSULTANT:

You still can't use it?

WORKSHOP PARTICIPANT:

Unfortunately, no. He says *his* boss might not like it.

Being products of our more mature selves, Corporate Bogeys have several characteristics that distinguish them from the earlier and more fearsome generations we'll be looking at shortly. For one thing, they always have names: "My boss," "the board," "this company," "our president," "others in the department," or even "John Polovski" or "Mary Beth Anderson." The older Bogeys have to share a common alias, "someone" (who "might").

Being more concretely conceived, Corporate Bogeys may also be more real. Since joining the company we may have learned from experience that, if we write a memo in a certain way, John Polovski not only *might,* but in fact *probably will,* come down on us. Given a known choice between fighting and losing, or complying and perhaps winning, we are wise to adapt. Thus, instead of always embodying generalized, phobic responses, Corporate Bogeys are sometimes reactions to actual behaviors of individuals. They can be, in other words, ongoing communications blocks rather than irrational fears.

CONSULTANT:

(*Puzzled, looked from one young woman to the other. The two worked closely together in the same office and had paired off in the training room for a letter writing project.*) You've both written excellent letters. But why are you both making these little, obvious errors. Uncrossed t's, undotted i's, conspicuous misspellings?

YOUNG WOMAN:

Oh, we always do that. Our boss is what you call a "compulsive editor." He always has to change something. If we don't leave some little mistakes for him to correct in our letters, he *might* screw up something important.

Though some Corporate Bogeys are comparatively innocuous, as a class they are costly. Attempts to appease the Corporate Bogeys motivate several expensive communications practices. For instance, they are responsible for the CYA, or PYA, traditions (cover—or protect—your ass) in organizational writing. That is, they are behind the many memos that should never have been written—the ones circulated in order to assure that the writer will have something in the files to defend himself with because John P. someday might call him to account. They also account for the "smoke screens," the memos carefully crafted in anticipation of failure—the ones intended to demonstrate, if something goes wrong, that the writer was certainly not the one responsible. And the Corporate Bogeys are also to blame for the "cloud," the memo so vaguely written it can later be squeezed to yield almost any interpretation that will lend comfort to its author.

The next war story recounts a time when, during a sales call, Consultant listened while a manager kowtowed to a Corporate Bogey.

Consultant Has a Talk with Manager, Special Projects

"I've reviewed your technical writing workshop and think it would be a good course for our staff to attend . . . with one qualification."

"Oh?"

"The part about putting the recommendations near the beginning of a report, right after the introduction and before the discussion. I don't want you to teach our people to do that."

"Oh?"

"That's right. I know some experts think the practice is acceptable, but I don't. Everyone should put their recommendations at the end of a report, where they belong."

"Oh?"

"The practice of putting the recommendations first only encourages lazy management. If the recommendations sound okay, managers might just approve them without even reading the rest of the report."

"Oh?"

"Besides, there's no need to put the recommendations at the beginning. Whenever I get a report from one of my people, I first read the introduction; then I turn to the back and look for the recommendations; then I read the rest of the report."

"Ohhh!"

The Client Gets Its Corporate Bogeys Organized

"Before you do any training for us, you need to be familiar with our corporate writing guidelines. Can we schedule a meeting for next week?"

Later, as Consultant's client base expanded, the obligatory meeting to explain the organization's legislated writing practices—the "company style manual"—would become a routine event; but this first invitation to one puzzled, even concerned, him.

What were the corporate guidelines? he worried. Would the trainees know them? If they already had guidelines, why were they bringing him in? Perhaps to teach their guidelines?

Most worrisome, what if the writing practices he intended to teach contradicted their guidelines? Consultant by then had enough experience in the Paper Wars to recognize a high probability—edging toward a sure bet—when he saw one.

But the guidelines, presented at the meeting by a young woman from the public relations department, turned out to be harmless, just a list of "words we don't use." The company was in business to achieve *earnings,* not *profits.* It was a utility that never had *power failures,* only *temporary service interruptions;* and people who did not pay their bills, rather than having their *power cut off,* had their *service suspended.* *Accidents* were *unavoidable incidents; mistakes* were *unfortunate judgments; I* and *we* were always *the Company.*

Being a worrier rather than a purist, Consultant had no philosophical objection to euphemisms. When feelings are running high, people can get into enough trouble without being careless in their choice of words. But he winced at the task ahead of him. The client organization, by acknowledging in print the power of its Corporate Bogeymen, and by installing as corporate policy the practices thought necessary to placate them, had publicly confirmed for its employees that their first responsibility as writers was to *be careful.*

The Profession Bogeys

We must now venture a look at the Profession Bogeys, an earlier generation of Bogeymen born at a younger time when the psyche of the individual, less experienced and formed, is more susceptible to the influence of others, more malleable to externally imposed images of how he or she is required to behave. These can be dangerous waters. The person who previously took pleasure in what I said about Corporate Bogeys may now suddenly turn pale and strike out. Before, I was exposing foolishness; now I risk being seen as attacking truth. Chuckling at some pointless practice the boss told us to *do* is one thing; questioning what our professors taught us to *be* is quite another.

I think I would be wise to start with a war story.

Consultant told me the project was the first ever to give him an unobscured view of a Profession Bogeyman. The client, a regional planning commission, was an example of an interesting kind of organizational structure that has had a brief life and is now disappearing. The mid-20th century first created a plethora of new technological jobs, and only later created new professions to fill them. In the interim, the new positions were taken up by generalists and by specialists trained in other fields who learned, on the job, how to play the new roles. As the needed professionals started to come off the university assembly lines, they occupied positions subordinate to the first comers. The result was an organization consisting of schooled specialists working under the direction of managers who, though experienced (and often wise) did not have equivalent training. Such organizations are becoming rare today, with the technocrats grown up and moving into the executive positions.

The agency involved in this story was created a couple of decades ago when a group of small town and rural municipal jurisdictions decided to get together and do some planning. Otherwise they were likely to be swallowed up, socially and economically, by a city that was growing rapidly in their midst. But no one had yet invented professional planners, so they had to start off by hiring talented amateurs to operate their new regional planning commission.

One of the original "amateurs" who was now director of the commission, a man with 20 years' experience in planning, sat behind the desk explaining the assignment to Consultant. "Our staff consists of people with degrees in such diverse fields as Economics, Sociology, Transportation, Agriculture, and Resource Management. We've been given the job of producing a regional plan that will guide the growth in the area surrounding the city for the next 30 years. The study is intended to be used by local councils, developers, community groups, journalists, and such. Our people have just finished a five-year study of the region, and now they have to get together and write the plan. But we've run into a few problems. So we decided to hire a part-time editorial consultant to help us keep on track with the writing. Are you interested in the job?"

As he became more skilled in his work, Consultant would develop antennae that were increasingly alert to words like "we've been having a few problems," and more sensitive to the tightening of the voice that often accompanied them. But he now presumed he had simply run into another case of professionals, assigned to write for the general public, who were bound up in BoG. He had ready-made answers to that problem.

BoG was indeed a major problem for the planners. But Consultant soon discovered the real reason he'd been hired. The young professional staff had taken the bit in their teeth and were in the process of creating a monster. The director, not being able to dissuade them, hoped Consultant could.

In Consultant's first meeting with the team doing the writing, the young project leader explained what they intended.

PROJECT LEADER:

> The regional plan will consist of two levels of reports. The first level will be eight primary reports on such topics as transportation, subdivision, and manufacturing. These will constitute the regional plan per se and will be released to the public.

CONSULTANT:

And the second level of reports?

PROJECT LEADER:

Those are the technical reports. Each primary report will be backed up by three to twelve technical reports that will contain the results of our research and our study data.

CONSULTANT:

Do I understand correctly? The technical reports won't be published?

PROJECT LEADER:

That's right. They'll be available here in the planning commission's files.

CONSULTANT:

May I ask a dumb question?

PROJECT LEADER:

Certainly.

CONSULTANT:

If the technical reports aren't going to be published, why are you writing them?

PROJECT LEADER:

Oh, we thought that would be obvious to a professional like yourself. *Someone might* question the information and conclusions in the primary reports. We have to be prepared to present the research that supports them.

Behind the decision to write and file a tall stack of unnecessary technical reports lurked a classic Profession Bogeyman—a specter born in the minds of young professionals in training as they read the cryptic comments in the margins of their returned term papers: *Can you back this up? Upon what evidence is this conclusion based? What reasons can you offer to justify saying this?* They had accepted the fact that *someone might* insist they demonstrate their professional orthodoxy. And they were fully prepared to divert the resources of the planning commission for months to write unnecessary reports that would assure their own peace of mind. The objections of the director could be easily dismissed, of course. Not being a professional himself, he didn't understand the importance of backing up one's conclusions with hard data.

As things worked out, of the approximately three dozen technical reports originally planned, only one came to be written. Unlike the others, which would have contained only a rehash of data taken from government publications, it presented the methodology and results of an original questionnaire-based survey the staff had designed to poll the region's residents. Because it constituted a new contribution to "the literature" of rural/urban planning, it enjoyed modest circulation and proved helpful to a number of other similar agencies.

The Profession Bogeys are the embodiment of people's anxieties about how they will be perceived by peers and experts in their own field. Born in the gap between C— and an A+, feeding on our awareness of all those "seminal" books we never got around to reading (or read but didn't understand), they can browbeat even recognized authorities.

Fear of Profession Bogeys accounts for a number of characteristic BoG phenomena: The determined use of insider jargon and acronyms, for instance, even when the intended audience is nonprofessional. Elaborately constructed technical justifications in response to simple questions. The insistence that every problem is more complicated than it needs to be. The habit of hedging every statement. ("It would appear that the highest gust was recorded at approximately 118.3 m.p.h." "There is a probability that the fire in the shed is what may account for the house burning down.") These Bogeys also assure resistance to new practices suggested by outsiders such as writing consultants, people who obviously can't comprehend the importance and complexity of the professional rituals.

One of the most cumbersome features of "professional" BoG is the dogged insistence that the reader must listen to the writer's whole case before being told what point the document is intended to make. The assumption seems to be that the writer, in order to prove himself "correct," must justify his thinking by trying to lead the reader through step-by-step to a conclusion, as in a school lab report. (A true professional, however, makes informed statements, then explains them knowledgeably.)

Even those who have distanced themselves from the local Bogeys haunting their corporation may keep a death grip on their Profession BoG and its associated writing practices. It's their first line of defense against the criticism they *might* hear from their peers if they risk departing from established ways.

Overheard on the Elevator

"What do you mean, my writing is too complicated? This memo is on a complicated subject."

"My point exactly. The more complicated the content, the clearer and more direct the style has to be."

"Good luck selling that one to my boss! . . . But suppose, then, the content is simple. Should the style be complicated?"

"That would be silly."

"In my department we do it all the time."

Senior Engineer Invents Another Never

This war story illustrates what can happen when a person tries to make others worship at the altar of his own profession's spooks.

Consultant found the writing strange. He thought he had seen BoG in all its manifestations, but what was happening on the page before him was new and exotic. And slippery too. He would glimpse a hint of what a passage might mean, then it would elude him, lost in some phrasing he could not account for.

Consultant was seated with a recently formed group called the planning task force. Bright, junior people, their job was to make research-based assumptions about where future trends might take the corporation and prepare reports on the problems and opportunities likely to result. They worked under the direction of a management committee composed of senior representatives from every department.

The meeting had been arranged by the president after he received the task force's first report. The president told Consultant he was impressed by the amount and apparent quality of the information in the report, but he and the board of directors were left curious to know what the task force was trying to tell them. After reading the document, Consultant could understand why.

To establish a starting point from which to work in the meeting, Consultant asked the task force leader to explain what seemed to be a key sentence in the report. We'll pick up the conversation at that point.

CONSULTANT:

Your explanation sounds great. Clear, simple, direct. Why don't you say that?

LEADER:

You mean, just write down the same words I'd use to explain the idea verbally? That doesn't sound like writing a report to me.

CONSULTANT:

Sure it is. The whole point is to get your idea communicated to the reader, as clearly and simply as you can. All you have to say in the report is what you just told me, "Within ten years, this company will likely. . . ."

LEADER:

> *(Interrupting.)* Oh no! We can't use the word *will* in our reports.

CONSULTANT:

> What?

LEADER:

> We can't use the word *will*.

CONSULTANT:

> Let's take this from the top, slowly. Your job is to study the *future*, to draw deductions about *future* trends, and then to report to the people who run this corporation on what they can probably expect . . . in the *future*. And you can't use *will*, the auxiliary verb the English language uses to signal the *future* tense?

LEADER:

> That's right. At our group's initial organizing meeting, the member of our managing committee from the engineering department made it very clear that we were *never* to use the word *will* in our reports. He said that *will* implies certainty that something *will happen*. He says we're not prophets who can predict the future; we can only offer educated guesses about what *might* happen in the future.

A Profession Bogeyman must have smiled down beneficently, happy to be appeased. Meanwhile the president and the board were scratching their heads, wondering what had gone wrong with their attempt to assure the future did not catch them off guard.

The Truth about All BoG, Profession BoG Included

Documents written in BoG are understood only by the person who wrote them, at the time of writing. Everyone else has to puzzle out what they *probably mean*.

It's not a matter of professionals who understand BoG and laypersons who don't. It's a matter of professionals being able to make educated guesses, while laypersons have to make *un*educated guesses, about what the writer may have meant to say.

The School Bogeys

The subject of the School Bogeys must be approached with trepidation. They are the oldest, least yielding and most vindictive. Products of our child selves, they were invented long ago in a vain attempt to find safety and conditional love in the alien world of omniscient, omnipotent adults. They brook no challenges, allow no appeals. They lay claim to the deepest core of linguistic certitude in ourselves. If we can't trust the admonitions of our School Bogeys, nothing, we feel, can protect us from what *might* happen if we err.

While blind obeisance to the Profession Bogeys accounts for much of the silliness in the Paper Wars, terror of the School Bogeys accounts for their viciousness. So I'm going to proceed cautiously, again starting with one of Consultant's war stories.

One of his associates once had a skirmish with some School Bogeys when she walked into a meeting with a purchasing committee. She found them hostile. They had gathered not to weigh the proposal from Consultant's firm, but to attack her for presuming to offer her services as a writing instructor. *Two words*, they said, had been consistently misspelled in the proposal, one being their company's name.

Misspellings and typos, the scourge of anyone who risks sending out written documents, are a special embarrassment to people in Consultant's profession. But in this case Consultant did not feel apologetic, even in the face of irate School Bogeys. If people want to create a corporate name by spelling a familiar word in an exotic way, fine; but they should accept their fate—they must forever spell out the word when talking over the phone. Having themselves chosen to "misspell" the word, they should have taken extra care to inform Consultant's office when they called asking for the proposal. And as to *appendixes,* the second word that raised the ire of the committee's School Bogies, it is correctly spelled as either *appendices* or *appendixes*—as a member of the committee discovered when he left the meeting room to check a dictionary.

Consultant's associate was forgiven (and subsequently did some excellent work for the client). But she left the meeting feeling as though she had been stopped by a policeman and scolded for *almost* committing a traffic violation.

The School Bogeys Attack Consultant for Daring to Be Different

Years ago Consultant received a letter with no formal salutation. Instead of preceding the letter with "Dear Mr. Consultant," the writer opened the first sentence with the words, "Thank you, Mr. Consultant, for contacting us about. . . ."

Consultant was impressed. Mildly excited, even. He knew from the questions people ask in training courses that some worry about writing letter salutations. "What's more acceptable, 'Dear Sir' or 'Dear Mr. Jones'?" "What if I don't know whether the reader is a man or woman; do I say 'Dear Sir or Madame'?" "I don't like calling strangers 'Dear'; it's even worse when I'm writing to someone I know and hate."

Consultant always tried to reassure people: "It doesn't matter what you say in the salutation. It's just a conventional part of the letter and nobody reads it anyway."

Some refused to take comfort. They were sure that, being an expert, he knew the *correct* way to write the salutation, but for some reason was keeping it to himself.

But here, in the letter before him, was a perfect solution: Dispense with the formal salutation altogether and address the reader by name in the first sentence. The new practice would avoid the discomforts of "Dear." More important, it would result in letters that were more effective. Previously the salutation had been only a dead space. Now it could be a high impact way of personalizing letters and creating an immediate focus on the reader and his or her interests. It would also provide infinite variety. "Congratulations, Ms. Smith, for. . . ." "We were pleased to hear, Mr. Jones, that you have. . . ." "We're releasing a new product next month, Mr. Doe. Here's your copy of. . . ."

Certainly Consultant did not intend to launch a crusade to get the new salutation generally adopted in business. If Paper Wars veterans have learned nothing else, they know to stand and fight only for practices that make a major difference. It would be dumb for him and his associates to risk neutralizing their considerable arsenal against BoG by giving holdouts an excuse to dig deep trenches in defense of a minor issue. People could invent enough Red Herrings on their own without his volunteering some.

He did, however, immediately install the first-sentence salutations as standard practice in his own firm.

Not all his colleagues were comfortable with the change. They wondered if it was worth the risk. Some of their clients, especially those of a more cautious bent, might see the practice as "trendy" and "unbusinesslike."

His response: "First-sentence salutations help in writing better letters because they replace something dead with something alive. We do not, as most of our competitors do, promise *safety* by helping perpetuate traditional practices; instead, we promise clients *effectiveness* by helping them install newer, more modern ways of communicating. If we are going to ask people to risk the ire of the Bogeys, we have to demonstrate that we're not afraid of them ourselves. Besides, if the 'experts' can't innovate, no one can."

So his company began writing first-sentence salutations. Over the years they've heard a few positive comments on the practice and the occasional dubious remark. The author of a textbook, for example, wrote to say his editor objected to the practice, but he had already been using it himself and felt vindicated by Consultant's example. But Consultant never received enough feedback to determine whether many of his firm's clients even noticed the practice.

In one exceptional case, however, his company was emphatically dumped on. An associate in a distant city called, distraught. "A new training director has been hired by the Fudge Corporation, and he just cancelled the pilot workshop we were going to run next month."

"Why?"

"He told me he'd seen the covering letter we sent with our proposal. In his words, 'Anybody who doesn't even know the correct way to begin a business letter is obviously not qualified to teach writing to our staff.' I told you those new salutations were going to get us into trouble someday."

The letter had aroused deep fears in the new training director. His School Bogeys would tolerate no tinkering with the "correct" ways.

(The client, by the way, was not lost. The Fudge Corporation VP who had been sponsoring the project from the beginning overruled the new training director when he learned of the cancellation. A solid training program followed.)

The issue that needs to be looked at is not the specific writing practices people might object to, but the intensity of the emotions—even the self-righteous certitude—that can charge their reactions when another writer makes choices that differ from ones they might make. We'll have to do considerable digging into our pasts to learn where the School Bogeymen came from and why we are so frightened of them.

How We Ingested Our School Bogeys

If there is a first sponsor and consistent champion of the School Bogeys that inhabit our minds, it is the English Teacher. I'm not speaking of specific English teachers we've known and admired. Miss Abercrombie, who loved both her language and her pupils, worked hard and honestly at bringing them together. We shouldn't blame Coach Rohn either; he ended up teaching English only because his study hall assignment conflicted with football practice. They both did the best they could with the system they were given to work with.

But the English Teacher, as a concept, is almost archetypal. Usually a female personification, she is a whispering voice in all of us. "Be careful!" "Don't make a mistake!" "Are you sure you're not breaking any rules?" "You never did figure out the difference between. . . ." Fear of the English Teacher within causes many otherwise sensible executives to go to battle on the side of their School Bogeys, defending the indefensible and perpetuating the very writing practices that cause their most serious communications problems.

Corporate power still tends to be vested in people who were schooled in, and often believe deeply in, the system known nostalgically as "Reading, Riting, 'n Rithmetic." Those who champion the old ways, with their emphasis on drill, rules, and correction, seem to misremember their effects. The traditional grammar-based English courses taught permanent lessons, but not always good ones. They did much that made people grow up to distrust the very literacy that schooling was intended to help them develop. The child in each of us does not remember all those rules—nor all those exceptions. The child remembers only that there were a lot of rules and exceptions; that he or she cannot remember most of them; and that the teacher insisted that people who do not know the rules are doomed to speak and write incorrectly. Thus are School Bogeys born.

I'm not blaming our teachers. They were stuck with a badly faulted system for teaching language skills. The old-fashioned English course had acquired, over the years, so many unexamined—even unexpressed—objectives that both teachers and students were confused about what was to be achieved. Did English instruction have a social purpose? That is, was it primarily intended to inculcate the language behaviors of the white, educated middle-class? Or was its purpose reformation, to achieve in English a latinate precision that no living language (including the one spoken by the Romans) had ever demonstrated? Did people study English grammar in order to understand how the language worked or to learn what errors to avoid? Was the purpose of composition to teach people to write useful documents, or just "correct" documents? Or, for that matter, were English courses simply an adult plot to force young people to read dull, difficult books that were supposedly good for them?

Traditional English instruction was loaded with ambiguities of purpose. But one objective, *correction,* was always clear to everyone. English class was the place where people's language behaviors, both written and oral, were criticized in elaborate detail.

The tradition endures. Textbooks offer only general guidance on how to write well, but they list in detail all the supposed errors that can be made. Recent publications on business writing scold executives for the same mistakes their teachers scolded them for years ago. And writing courses, usually being light on the heavy stuff and heavy on the light stuff, catalogue the language rituals that will, they promise, preserve us from our Bogeys; but they teach little about how to create a report that will help our boss make a major decision, or about how to respond to a complaint letter without making the customer even more angry.

Even today, many executives are reluctant to approve a writing workshop for their employees unless first assured that it will teach people "what they are doing wrong."

So if people learned nothing else from their English teachers, they learned to be careful. Safety lay not in communicating well but in writing cautiously, not in having something to say but in avoiding error. One can understand, therefore, why today's executive might consider writing a dangerous activity. At the core of the urge to use BoG is the adult's understandable reluctance to risk exposure to the criticism experienced as a pupil and student.

People's on-the-job learning can be effectively blocked by these quiet fears. They can be frustrated, when reading, by a noncommunicative writing practice. Yet if that practice seems to conform to something remembered from school, they will defend and perpetuate it. Many mature, intelligent, and powerful people will argue that they "can't" or "shouldn't" use a perfectly good word because a teacher once, for a reason no longer remembered, red-penciled it in a school essay.

Like most fears, those stirred by the School Bogeys can motivate contradictory and dysfunctional behaviors. Managers may complain, for example, about the lack of clarity in other people's reports, then criticize their own people for using language that is "too clear." Those in power frequently send subordinates to training programs to learn to write better, then methodically edit out any subsequent changes that appear in their memos and reports. Business writing consultants know, when called in to help improve an organization's writing, they will spend much of their initial time listening to explanations why people in that organization "have to" continue writing exactly as they have always written.

The Bogeymen Scare the Bosses Away

The three generations of Bogeys not only conspire to assure organizations write BoG, they actively resist efforts to introduce CleaR as well. They attempt to keep secret the real reasons people write BoG by trying to frighten off managers who venture too near the truth. Whispering secret inner warnings, they make executives fearful that, if they publicly come to grips with organizational writing problems, they might expose deficiencies of their own.

When Consultant first goes into an organization to teach workshops, he offers to help managers take control of the change process by conducting a two-hour session on business writing values and criteria. In trying to schedule such sessions, he has discovered the two-part Law of Manager Participation:

  a. Managers will agree to attend a session on writing, but only if the date is set far enough away.
  b. When the time comes, they won't show up.

Thus Consultant's management sessions, when they occur at all, usually take place long after the training has started. And many of the managers who earlier agreed to come are represented by subordinates delegated to "report what was said" in the meeting.

The Lits and Alits Go to School and Learn Their Bogeys

A tendency to either verbal or symbolic thought seems to be genetically determined, a given for each individual. But what nature decrees, nurture shapes. Although lits and alits have both ingested School Bogeys, alits seem to believe more deeply in and are likely to be more afraid of theirs, a fact not surprising considering that school was a much different experience for alits than it was for lits.

Teaching is a highly verbal activity (at least the way it is usually practiced). Therefore teachers—even teachers in the symbolic disciplines—tend to have a strong verbal orientation. And of course those with the strongest verbal orientation have always been the most serious about teaching English.

When today's senior executives were in school, most teachers did not know that some of their pupils had different minds than they did. They just thought their classes were divided between the smart kids and the dumb kids, not the verbal kids and the nonverbal kids. The fluent were rewarded with smiles; those who mumbled and stumbled were punished with frowns. One child—when his grammar was corrected in midsentence—took the instruction with good will. Another, who already had enough trouble putting his thoughts into words without being interrupted and distracted by the teacher, became frustrated and withdrawn.

In school most alits learned—and as adults will readily confess—that they were "not good in English." Their natural disaptitude for verbal expression was twisted into a chronic sense of inadequacy and failure. For them using the language—especially in its irrevocable written form—came to be a dangerous activity that was almost inevitably punished by criticism. Therefore alits have a heightened awareness of all the bad things that *might* happen when a person has to write something down.

I'm not suggesting that lits got off free. For one thing, being a lit does not, in fact, mean that one is smart. It means only that one is more likely to be fluent. So lits, too, made mistakes of expression and content that earned them red marks. Even the brightest and most talented rarely escaped unscathed. If we could somehow scrutinize all the "A" essays written in all the English classes everywhere, we would find very few that did not have at least one or two "errors" marked. Perhaps we'd find only a comma changed to a semicolon; or a semicolon changed to a comma; or three words struck out and replaced by one. But we would find some signs of "correction." English teachers—whether instructing pupils in school, students in college, or adult professionals in industry or government—do not acknowledge that anyone in the classroom has achieved full competency as a writer. Ever.

So lits are not uninfected; they are simply less affected. Their loyalties to the School Bogeys are usually not as fierce, and they are not likely to invest as much in placating them. Lits are also more open to realities that contradict the Mighty Nevers. They can face the fact, for instance, that in spite of what their English teacher said, skilled practitioners of the language often split infinitives in order to emphatically place an adverb. They do not pale when told that ending sentences with prepositions is an old practice that good writers regularly adhere to. And they don't never believe that old nonsense about two negatives communicating a positive. Such a blatant instance of nonstandard grammar would be damagingly distracting in a business document; but most lits grasp that it is several degrees removed from mortal sin.

Yet lits, while perhaps less loyal to the School Bogeys, may be just as adamant as alits in standing up for the Profession and Corporate Bogeys. They too can be jealous about maintaining their membership privileges in the Club.

Ultimately, the most damaging thing that gets taught during school may be permission to allow oneself righteous and indignant outbursts in the presence of language practices that depart from one's own; that is, permission not only to overstate the case when differences of opinion arise, but to stamp one's foot and declare practices of others to be "incorrect" or "unacceptable." Some systems seem to take more comfort in absolutes than others. North Americans who have occasion to converse with their British counterparts are familiar with the intelligent and amiable conversation that is jerked to a halt by an expression of disdain at a difference in pronunciation, for example.

Lits may have fewer Bogeys than alits; and they may be less afraid of them; yet they are just as likely to respond with objectionable certitude when their own writing values are challenged. Offended by the fact that BoG sounds pretentious, sometimes even silly, some lits have had the bad manners to accuse BoG writers, inaccurately, of being pretentious, even silly people.

Lits' effectiveness in the Paper Wars is often compromised as a result. They may find, for example, that in trying to help an alit who, in attempting to placate his Profession Bogeys, has elaborately argued a strong case into a weak one, their very intensity may assure he digs in his heels and insists the document be sent out unchanged. And when a traditional cautious practice—such as trying to "soften up" someone to prepare him for bad news—predictably intensifies the reader's irritation and anger, the lesson the writer might have learned may be drowned out by the righteousness in the voice of some lit saying "I told you so."

The schools are to blame for making the Paper Wars so bloody. They taught people that, when the issue is a difference of opinion about language, it's okay to fight dirty.

Which Audience Are You Writing For?

Rather than crafting documents intended to meet the needs of real, external readers, those who write BoG create documents intended to placate the hypothetical criticisms of their own inner spooks. Our Bogeys are a composite of painful memories—perhaps several sharp-tongued teachers, two or three dogmatic professors, and probably a succession of bosses who were themselves bedeviled by Bogeys. Often the proxy for all these background audiences is the writer's current boss, who cautiously edits people's work to assure his own hobgoblins are not offended.

Those who understand about Bogeys and recognize their influence have an advantage in the Paper Wars. They are less likely to be fooled about what is really going on, less likely to go off chasing chimeras that others conjure up to hide their inner terrors.

Had Consultant discovered the Bogeys earlier he might have been more consistent in helping his clients. He might, for example, have done a better job with the Offshore Drilling Manual. Consultant did not understand that Senior Engineer was proud of the manual, believing he and his writers had competently fulfilled their primary responsibility, satisfying their Profession Bogeys. Senior Engineer just wanted an English teacher's assurance that no one could detract from their accomplishment by uncovering, in the manual, offenses against the School Bogeys. Then Consultant marched in and announced his own Bogeys—those aroused when the intended readers are not served. Senior Engineer had heard of such Bogeys before, but he probably felt little compulsion to honor them. He had always been punished for making errors or for failing to be meticulous, not for writing documents that people could not understand.

Likewise Consultant might have been able to explain to the VP why the Professor's article on the six writing styles seemed so comforting. It appeased the executive's Profession Bogeys by acknowledging the complexity of the writing task. Surely a set of practices so elaborate in execution and requiring such subtle judgments about variables is immune to attack from insufficiently informed outsiders.

Thus an awareness of the Bogeys is a big help in picking our way through the minefields of the Paper Wars. But we must *never* attempt to use that knowledge as a weapon. If we ever try to win an argument by waiving someone's Bogey in his face all hell will break loose, just as surely as if he waves one of our favorites at us.

We don't admit to our deeper Bogeys. Being a product of childhood fears, they make us feel childish and fearful. They are dark cellars and spiders; big green things and cold squishies with teeth hiding under the bed. They are irrational; not founded in fact; and indefensible. So we disguise them behind careful rationalizations—behind elaborate explanations of the special constraints under which business writers, especially in our own organization, must write.

The usual charge is that so much writing is so bad because people in business and government are insensitive to their readers. Consultant insists, however, that people write badly because they are *too* sensitive to the *wrong* readers, their Bogeys—School, Profession, and Corporate. But once they exorcise their Bogeys and start thinking instead about the right readers—the real people who need their help— they find that they, and their organizations, start writing much better.

CHAPTER 5

PREPARING TO WIN

*The part of us that reads is
straightforward. It just wants to get
the desk cleared and go home feeling
the day has been worth living.*

Mobilizing Our Best Ally

Victories are never accidental; they must be prepared for.
Consultant says that none of us should risk launching an
attack on BoG and its sponsoring Bogeys until completing
one critical step. We must first mobilize our truest ally, the
Reader within ourselves. We must each get in touch with
that voice, and we must learn to hear, and believe, what he
or she has been trying to tell us all along.

We'll now set out on a short search for the Inner Reader.

Telling Our Reader from Our Writer

"Split personality" has never been a valid psychiatric term;
but anyone who thinks it doesn't exist in the Paper Wars is
going to get blindsided until he's punchy. Each of us has
within two separate selves: our Reader, who uses written
documents; and our Writer, who produces them. Talk about
a schizoid pair!

Let's listen in on a conversation between Ernest's
Reader and Joe's Writer.

ERNEST'S READER:

> This progress report really confused me. I didn't even figure out
> until half way through which project you were talking about.

JOE'S WRITER:

I thought that would be obvious. This is the third report I've sent you. You assigned me to the project almost six months ago.

ERNEST'S READER:

I did? I mean, yes, I did. But I'm overseeing five other projects as well, and they're just a small part of my work. But tell me, what does this sentence mean? "The unfortunate possibility I mentioned in my previous report now appears likely to become a distinct probability."

JOE'S WRITER:

Oh, I thought that would be obvious too. That's when I warned you about the explosion.

ERNEST'S READER:

The explosion? You mean the one I was just discussing with the fire marshal and the insurance adjuster?

JOE'S WRITER:

That's the one.

ERNEST'S READER:

But you never warned me about any explosion.

JOE'S WRITER:

Sure I did. That's the sentence you just read.

ERNEST'S READER:

Why on earth should I interpret, "The unfortunate possibility I mentioned in my previous report now appears likely to become a distinct probability," as meaning the plant was about to blow up?

JOE'S WRITER:

It should have been obvious. See, right here in my second report—the one I sent you two months ago—I said, "The concern I mentioned in my first report is increasingly becoming a possibility."

ERNEST'S READER:

> *(After a pause.)* Okay, I'll bite. What concern did you mention in your first report?

JOE'S WRITER:

> Surely you haven't forgotten. Fortunately I have a copy right here. . . . Let's see, it should be around page 18. . . . Yes, here it is. "As you are aware, the project will involve the use of materials which, if not properly handled, can be explosive. The situation will be carefully monitored and the appropriate parties will be informed should there be any cause for concern."

ERNEST'S READER:

> Why you . . . you . . . you . . . .

JOE'S WRITER:

> I don't know what you're so upset about. You approved all my reports and forwarded them to the Vice President. You didn't change a thing.

ERNEST'S WRITER (Cuts in):

> Oh, well, that's different. When a report is going to the VP, you don't just come right out and say things that will be obvious to him when he reads it.

We can easily tell our own Writer from our Reader, once we become aware of the two. Our Writer is the part of us that's scared. Our Reader is the part that's frustrated. Our Writer fears what the Bogeys *might* do if we stop writing BoG. Our Reader dislikes the bad impression other people *inevitably* make by continuing to write it. Our Reader is the part of us that finds everyone else's BoG irritating and pointless.

Eavesdropping on Our Writer and Our Reader

It would be instructive to listen in on conversations between our Writer and our Reader—if we could ever get them in the same room together.

"I'm not supposed to begin sentences with the words *because, and,* and *but.*"

"What do you mean, you're not supposed to? You and I see it done all the time in books and magazines."

"When writing bad news letters, I'm first supposed to soften up readers by saying positive things."

"Soften them up? You're trying to set them up. Don't you remember how ticked we were by the memo from the boss that told us what a wonderful job we were doing, then sprung the news that our budget was being cut?"

The Writer within the special projects manager insisted his engineers put their recommendations at the end of a report, "where they belong." His Reader then had to go looking for them.

The Reader says, "Here's a new way of beginning a letter that really impressed me. Let's start using it." His Writer refuses. "No, I'm not supposed to do it that way."

The Reader says, "Here's how we can write an emergency procedures manual that the drillers will understand." The Writer balks. "That's not how we were taught to write in engineering school."

"I can't say that. This is a formal report." "Formal report be damned. We Readers want to know what's going on."

What Our Readers Have Been Trying to Tell Us

Consultant has discovered the best way to help an organization mobilize to win the Paper Wars is to get its senior executives to sit down together. Then he gets *their Inner Readers to start talking to each other.* The experience is incredibly freeing for everyone concerned. Our Readers are sane, sensible, adult parts of ourselves. They can discuss change without blaming someone for its necessity, and they can focus on the positive and constructive.

But Consultant says he has never figured out a dependable way to get executives' Inner *Writers* to listen in while their *Readers* are discussing the BoG problem. Jointly their Readers, supporting each other in the conference room, will agree that writing has to change. They'll also agree on precisely what changes need to be made. But apparently their Writers Within start scolding them as soon as they walk out the door. Back at their offices, where the Bogeys are in charge, many executives get cold feet. Their Readers' firm resolve and good sense get shouted down the first time they consider writing a letter *differently,* or approving and forwarding a report a subordinate has written differently. Then their old BoG-protective behaviors resume control.

So I'm sorry. Consultant and I simply can't tell you how to get your Writer to listen to your Reader. That's a private victory each must win if we and our organizations are to write in a professional and competent way. We can report, though, *what your Writer will hear* if it ever does listen. Consultant and his associates have sat in attendance while the Readers of thousands of people explained what they want when they sit down to wade through a stack of letters, memos, and reports. Here are the two primary messages everyone's Reader has been trying to communicate to other people's Writer for years.

Help Me. I need your information and your guidance. Tell me what you think I should know and what decisions you believe I should make. Explain things for me. Make everything clear. Then I can make my own, grown-up judgments about whether we agree.

Don't Play Games with Me. Don't try to soften me up. Don't try to make me read and remember everything you want to say before telling me why I should even care. Don't treat me like someone who's prideful; quick to take offense; critical about the smallest detail; and itching to say no. I'm the same decent and (usually) reasonable person when sitting at my desk reading your report as I am in the meeting room or the coffee room. And remember, as a Reader I have no interest in trying to track my way through circumlocutions and ploys intended to protect you from your Bogeys. Your Bogeys are your problem, not mine.

When the Readers of managers are in charge and talking with each other, Consultant asks them: What do you want me to tell the Writers in your people? What do you most want them to *do* when they write a memo or report for you? The *Readers within senior executives*—industry to industry, agency to agency, large organization and small, in North America and abroad—*have been giving the same five answers for 20 years.*

1. *Have them tell me, right at the beginning, why they are writing.* If they want me to approve an expenditure; if they want me to attend a meeting; if they want me to reverse a decision; if they want me to read their memo and offer my opinion; even if they just want me to note the thing and file it; I need to know that first. Then I can listen to what the document says. And the more negative or troublesome their news may be, the more I need them to announce it in the first paragraph. I don't want to read clear to the end and then have something sprung on me.

2. *Tell them to explain things to me.* They should especially explain what seems so "obvious." Making me aware of the obvious is probably the reason for writing the memo or report in the first place. I've got plenty of work of my own to keep track of; they should never expect me to be on top of the details of their operation. But when there is something I *should* know, their job is to make sure I find out. I'm never offended when someone makes my work easier by delivering up information in an explicit, interpreted form I can understand immediately and put to use.

3. *I want them to use words I can understand. In fact, they should make mental pictures for me.* I want them to keep their language simple and concrete. Instead of saying "Market trends for appliances appear to be improving," they should say "People have started buying more appliances." I don't want to have to figure out what they mean by "An inclusive series of personal interviews was conducted at the management level in order to determine what should constitute the initial step." They should just say, "We asked all the managers what they thought we should do first." I have a mountain of reading every day. I don't have time for word puzzles.

4. *Tell them to give me all the information I need to do what they want, or to understand what they think I should know—and only that information.* A report should not read like a final examination in the subject. It's not a test of how much the writer knows. Nor should it be a collection of the odds and ends that happened to come to mind at the time of writing. Writers should plan each document by asking themselves, "If I had to make this decision, what would I want someone to tell me?" They then should select, from everything they might say, *only* the data that will help me; and then they should make sure I get *all* of it.

5. *Also remind them that I, too, am human.* I prefer to be addressed as a fellow member of the same species, not an automaton. Especially if the issue is troublesome, a constructive tone is important. When someone starts off with, "It has come to our attention . . . ," I feel like kicking him in the teeth. But if he starts with, "I'm sorry to be the bearer of bad news, but you need to know that . . . ," the disappointment is easier to swallow.

Consultant has been getting these five messages from people's Inner Readers, week in and week out, for years. The part of us that reads is straightforward. It just wants to get the desk cleared and go home feeling the day has been worth living.

* * * * *

Consultant, who's looking over my shoulder, has pointed out something I should tell you. If you hear inner voices clamoring, "Writing's *got* to be more complicated than that!" it's just your Bogeys fighting for their lives. When our Writers start listening to our Readers, our Bogeys begin to wither. Attention and obeisance are the only nourishment that keeps them alive.

Freeing Our Reading Selves

Our Writers learn to write by writing. But they usually come through the process bruised and battered because of the kind of feedback writing incites. Our ability, say, to make ourselves understood by *speaking* gives us steady flow of immediate feedback—the listener's words, facial expressions and even body language tell us whether we've communicated, and how well. Feedback on our writing, on the other hand, is always delayed and fragmented. It comes days or weeks following the act of writing itself, long after we've forgotten the experience of producing the document. And we seldom find out how the whole document succeeded; we get feedback only on the parts that happened to stir a response from the reader. Thus the comments written on a returned essay or report may be a truer reflection of the mood of the reader on the day it was read than the effectiveness of the writing. And feedback to writing is not only capricious, it is usually negative as well. The reader's comments will almost always name errors rather than point out successes. No wonder our Writer Within is such a cautious and fearful chap, so hesitant to try anything new.

Now for the good news. For every *minute* our *Writer* has spent receiving instruction in English class or has spent reviewing the comments others have written in our margins, our *Reader* has spent a *hundred hours*—perhaps a *thousand hours*—absorbing the written language privately and constructively. Since before we wrote our first sentence our Reader has been observing and learning; making deductions from the practices it sees other writers perform, then organizing those deduction into principles and filing them away in our memory banks.

We have in our minds a warehouse of understanding about how to use the language that is an essential part of our heritage as humans living in an organized society, and a very substantial area of that warehouse specializes in storing knowledge of how to use the language in its *written* form. Thus our Reader Within possesses most of the knowledge, and almost all of the *true* knowledge, each of us has about writing.

Our Inner Readers, like the rest of us, did most of their growing during childhood. Their vigor and strength varies. True illiterates, in fact, don't have a Reader. The tribesman wandering in from the desert is not only ignorant of what the words on signs say; he does not even know what they are. A young person who leaves school having been taught that reading is a boring, unpleasant chore to be done only under duress will as an adult be served by a puny weakling of a Reader. The child, on the other hand, who reads everything in sight, and then reads it again when nothing else is available, will grow up to have a lusty, brawling Reader who can shout down even a television set. A strong Reader is a first line defense against being manipulated by propaganda and misled by untruth. A society that does not read cannot be free.

But we can safely assume that you, the person holding this volume, has a vigorous, well-trained Reader. Otherwise you would not have picked up the book, let alone persisted this far. We can probably assume also that other people's Inner Writers (or perhaps your own) may not be performing to your satisfaction. You would not have bothered with the book if something wasn't troubling you about writing.

Having a strong Reader Within, then, you need not ask, "How can I (or we) ever know enough about writing?" You *already* know essentially everything you'll ever need in order to write fully competent business documents—and to help others write them. Your real question is, "Who holds the keys to my warehouse?" Your Reader has stored away more than ample knowledge there. But who controls access to it? Your Writer? Or your Bogeys?

Writers of BoG have trouble getting in touch with their own language awareness because their Bogeys let out only a few favorite, prescribed practices. They declare everything else to be something "you're not supposed to do," something that is "inappropriate to business and technical writing," and leave it locked up in the vaults.

People who use CleaR, on the other hand, are rich in practices they *can* use. Having discovered how to wrest the warehouse keys from their Bogeys and turn them over to their Inner Writers, they have an overflowing account of positive writing practices to draw upon.

When those who write CleaR prevail, the organization becomes literate. Thus the way to create a literate organization is not to dump more odds and ends of knowledge and correction in; it is to release from the bondage of the Bogeys the vast knowledge resources already waiting there. CleaR is free; and freeing; it is, in fact, freedom from older, darker parts of ourselves that can keep us from being all we want to be.

Bringing Together Our Writer and Reader

In extolling the importance of "Getting it all together," the pop psych of the 70s was describing our primary psychological task as adults: integration of our various selves. Just as the individual who aspires to the freedom and self-actualization of CleaR must integrate the Writer Within with the Reader Within, so must the organization. As long as the Writer and Reader are in conflict—as long as they are demanding contradictory accomplishments of the organization's written communications—the Paper Wars will continue unabated and BoG will endure.

But before either personal or corporate integration is possible, the Writer Within must grow up and catch up. It must first become healthy through *unlearning;* that is, it must cast out its Bogies and heal its fears. Only then will it be open to learn from, and fuse with, the Reader Within and the communications skills the Reader has waiting.

Let's keep this goal of integration in mind while we ponder, in the next chapter, a conundrum: why does the *dis*integration that sponsors BoG continue to rule the written communications of so many organizations in spite of the frustrations, errors, and inefficiencies it causes? The answer, according to Consultant, is that many people in business and government, attacked for how they write, and afraid to write differently because of the even more dangerous attacks they *might* suffer, look for someplace to hide.

CHAPTER 6

THE HIDING PLACES

*People seem to feel safer imitating
the mediocre than the exemplary.*

The Professor Shows People Where to Hide

Consultant likes to tell the story of a one-day education meeting, focusing on communications, attended by some 150 petroleum engineers. Four speakers were on the agenda. One, an engineering consultant, talked about specification writing. He spent his hour and a half trying to explain, to the people in the farther two-thirds of the room, what they would see if they could make out the tiny print on his detailed overhead transparencies. The speaker on public speaking was a lawyer who a short time later became a high-profile candidate for public office. His talk was enthusiastic and informative, though perhaps the style he demonstrated was overly aggressive, given his audience. They seemed to want to know how to survive giving a speech, not how to make it rousing. Consultant spoke on letter and memo writing. He's never mentioned the deficiencies of his own performance.

The topic of report writing was assigned to a prominent Professor of Engineering from the local university. He used his hour and a half to explain that people wanting to become competent report writers must do three things.

First, they have to stop reading all newspapers and but a few (rather literary sounding) magazines. Ordinary publications, it seems, taint minds less rigorous than the Professor's by presenting too many examples of bad writing practices.

Second, people must read at least six of the ten books on writing reviewed by the Professor. None of them sounded very palatable even to Consultant, who, one might think, would take a professional interest in the subject matter.

Third, the attendees at the meeting were told they must be patient. They were assured that, having stopped exposing themselves to bad models, and having ploughed their way through the required books, they would make no detectable improvements in their writing for two years, at least. That was the minimum time the Professor would allow for people to develop competencies that someday might approach (one would suppose) his own.

Consultant was not impressed. He thought the only message the Professor brought the 150 people attending was that they didn't have a hope of ever becoming adequate report writers.

The audience, however, was positive, even enthusiastic. During the luncheon the dining room buzzed with conversation about the Professor's speech. When Consultant suggested to a longtime acquaintance, the member of the organizing committee who had invited him to speak, that something might be awry with the Professor's approach, the man looked puzzled. "I suppose one could look at it that way. But I thought it was a good talk."

The engineers, rather than being discouraged by the Professor's sententious nonsense, took heart from it. They had come to the meeting expecting to be scolded for their bad reports. But the Professor hadn't scolded them. He had instead scolded journalists, people who after all should know better. In citing books no one had ever made them read, he justified their not being able to do what those books were supposed to teach. And his final service was to relieve them of responsibility for improving. To expect any working adult to give up the daily paper, to read a stack of boring books, and then to devote two unrewarding years to practicing without a sign of improvement, was clearly unrealistic. So they could continue writing just as they always had, but now with the assurance of an eminent member of their own profession that they were beyond reasonable redemption.

The engineers liked the Professor's speech because it confirmed that, for those who prefer to avoid the pain of improving either their own writing or their organization's, plenty of Hiding Places exist.

hide, hīd, *v.t.*—past *hid,* pp. *hidden* or *hid,* ppr. *hiding.* To conceal intentionally from sight; to prevent from being observed readily; to conceal from discovery; to secrete; to obstruct or block the view of; to conceal from knowledge or to maintain secrecy.

The three Hiding Places invoked by the Professor are familiar to those who fight BoG for a living. In criticizing newspapers and magazines, he was using *Let's look at other people's bad writing rather than our own.* In presenting his list of writing books, he was using *Let's not change our writing now; let's wait until we have more information on the subject.* And in declaring his two-year clause, he was using *Thank goodness the job is impossible; now we don't have to tackle it.*

The Hiding Places, which come in dozens of varieties, are the reasons people give to justify:

a. either not confronting BoG; or
b. confronting BoG in such ineffectual ways that their Bogeys aren't offended.

Let's look at some of the places people hide.

Computers, the Newest Hiding Place

When the full promise of electronic word processing came to be recognized, a sigh of relief went through the business world. "See, we told you we should hold off on doing anything about our bad writing. Now a technological solution has been invented." In the training room much the same argument can be heard. "What you're saying may have been true once, but now we write on computers."

Sorry. Computers have made only one major contribution to *better* written communication. Because they make writing and revising infinitely easier, they encourage more practice at both. Otherwise computers are only a secondary help. They can find misspelled words (but not other typos). By separating document editing on the screen from document production by the printer, they enable us to send out immaculate copy without tears. And since the introduction of the laser printers, even the most routine documents can have an eye-appeal impossible to achieve with the old keystrike machines. Otherwise computers and word processing software have given organizations only the ability to turn out more BoG, faster.

Computers have marvelously contributed to the work efficiency of us all. But the end product is still *writing*. What gets created and edited on the screen must, when spat out by the printer, make sense to a reader.

A recent item in the newspapers presented the results of a study conducted by a group promoting EDT, or electronic data transmission. They were puzzled, even disappointed, by what their survey revealed. Of the total messages (including telephone calls) transmitted by business and government, almost 80 percent were still in written form—despite the availability of the new electronic technology. If they conduct the survey again ten, twenty or thirty years from now, they will probably find little has changed. Data can be transmitted electronically, but *data is not information*. Data becomes information only when it has been sorted out, interpreted, organized into a case, and presented to another person as an explanation why she should accept a certain set of conclusions to be true or a particular course of action to be beneficial. That function, organizations have found, is best fulfilled by writing various kinds of documents (which, once written, can be transmitted electronically if one wishes).

So computers have made the physical act of writing much easier. But they have saved no one from having to write. And they have created some new, and sometimes surprising, problems of their own.

If you are a vice president who's been wondering why the writing crossing your desk has not in fact improved, even though people have had computers on their desks for close to a decade, the following war story may be revealing.

COURSE PARTICIPANT:

This Lazy Word Index you gave us really works. But we won't need it after the course. The computer analyzes our writing for us.

CONSULTANT:

The computer analyzes it?

COURSE PARTICIPANT:

Yeah. It gives us a score that indicates the reading level the document is written for—8th grade, 12th grade, university graduate, and so on.

CONSULTANT:

What does it actually measure?

COURSE PARTICIPANT:

I don't really understand the technical aspects of the program. But it has something to do with the length of sentences and the number of syllables in the words.

CONSULTANT:

Oh, sure, the old Fog Index. It's been around since the 1940s, and there are a number of variations of it circulating under different names. So someone has dusted it off and put it into a computer program. You say you're finding it helpful? How do you use it?

COURSE PARTICIPANT:

Well, as I said, it tells us the reading level of a memo or report. So when I write something for my people I try to stick to shorter sentences and avoid big words. I test what I write and keep revising it until I've got it down to about an 8th grade level.

CONSULTANT:

That's great! According to studies, the general population reads, on average, at about the grade six to eight level. But you said, "When I write for my people." What about when you write for other readers?

COURSE PARTICIPANT:

Oh, that's different. When I write a report for the VP, for instance, I keep adding big words and stretching out the sentences until I push the scale up into the university graduate range.

Hiding behind the School

If one Hiding Place is, *We don't have to do anything about bad writing now; the computer has taken care of the problem,* its cousin is, *We should wait; someday the schools will again start turning out people who can write.*

Fat chance. The teachers of the pupils presently in school belong to the second generation, merging into the third, that was raised on TV. If high schools are, by their own confession, having difficulty producing graduates who can *read* at a ninth grade level, we have little reason to assume they will shortly start teaching students to *write* at any adequate level of competency. Every indicator available suggests that the general literacy level of the population is declining rather than improving. (The new computer technology can be thanked for the only encouraging news to come from the schools. Children, now relieved of the finger-searing drudgery of writing by hand, are taking to writing earlier and with much more enthusiasm.)

As to the English departments in the universities, they can be expected to continue teaching expository writing with their noses held. Although some bright and dedicated university people take a serious interest in the subject, and although a few institutions have started offering degrees in the teaching of writing, the English faculties generally have long tolerated composition only for economic reasons. It fattens the budget by keeping departmental enrollments up (writing courses are usually required for graduation). Composition courses also provide a means of keeping graduate students gainfully employed while pursuing advanced degrees in literature, and they provide a captive market for textbooks written by professors (the only category of authors who have the power to require people to buy each others' books). But in terms of professional commitment, composition is a soot-smudged stepsister; the teaching of literature is the *raison d'etre* of English departments.

So there is little likelihood the universities will take an interest in improving the writing abilities of their end product, the people they graduate. They bemoan the fact that those who come to them from high schools are badly trained, but they seem satisfied to lecture at them and correct their papers for the appointed term or two, then send them on to professional courses, and eventual employment, with many of their writing faults intact. Though dedicated to their self-appointed mission of turning out "educated people" (as distinct from people who know how to do something useful), academics seem not to have considered that a demonstrated ability to read and write, in the eyes of taxpaying laypersons, might constitute minimum criteria for determining whether university graduates are in fact "educated."

Even the smattering of new interest the universities are taking in the teaching of writing is not especially promising. They are unlikely to change their fundamental teaching methodology, even though the lecture-assign-correct strategy has now proven its worth by turning out several successive generations of graduates with marginal writing competencies.

Thus universities produce graduates who cannot write; then business and government hire them and, in deference to the Bogeys, teach them how to write BoG. Both hide from the problem of bad writing by criticizing each other for it.

The Engineers Duck behind Their Sacred Cow

"No, we don't have any problems with writing. *We use the bullet style.*"

Some years ago "point form," or the "bullet style," was proposed as a way to write memos and short reports. It has since become, in certain professions, *the* way to write them.

Point form is the practice of numbering each sentence in the document except the first and last. (Nowadays some writers use dots or dashes instead of numbers.) Originally it was the result of a conspiracy between those who don't like to write and those who don't like to read. The writer, by making a series of discrete statements, more or less in the order they come to mind, can knock off a memo in the shortest time possible. And by numbering each sentence sequentially, he can not only create an impression of purposeful organization but also disguise the fact that the document consists entirely of bald statements presented in one-sentence, undeveloped paragraphs.

The recipient—who may have learned in school that the only purpose of reading is to get assignments done—often is a willing coconspirator. After simply letting the eyes slide over each neatly separated statement in order, he or she can claim to have "read" the memo. Thus point form is an admirable adaptation for getting two unpleasant tasks done with minimum pain, and people often insist they *have to* write it because their boss requires it.

Consultant has no philosophical quarrel with point form. He knows it can be a useful way of organizing steps in a user or procedures manual, or for setting off recommendations, or of presenting a few, clearly parallel major points. However, as a standard practice for organizing a whole document, point form has four failings:

1. It presents information in a form that cannot be readily remembered by readers.
2. It obliterates the distinction between major ideas and supporting details.
3. It makes the task of interpreting information much more difficult.
4. It hides the logical organization of the document.

The technique can be used effectively (as above) to separate and highlight a few parallel ideas that are of equal importance. However, if used as a habitual crutch for getting writing tasks out of the way, it is an assured method for turning out letters, memos, and reports that have little impact upon the reader.

As long as the memo or report says nothing worth paying much attention to, the bullet style is certainly a quick way to get it written, read, and into our files. But when communication matters—when readers need to remember information or to make important decisions based upon it—they should insist that writers adopt the old-fashioned practice of writing organized documents consisting of paragraphs, each of which should make a topic statement, then explain it.

The Economists Hide behind the Clerks

The prospective client, a federal agency that played a major role in helping politicians monitor the national economy, had a large staff of economists whose BoG was clogging the reporting process. When management requested the economists be trained to write reports that noneconomists could understand, the human resources development (HRD) manager called in Consultant.

HRD MANAGER:

> The economists are the core of our agency's operations. But our department finds them difficult to serve. Although they often approach us with requests for training, they are very

concerned about getting a sufficiently advanced program. They feel, given their professional backgrounds, that most training courses are too basic for them. So we want to find a serious writing program for them, not just another "here are the usual errors to avoid" course. How advanced is your workshop?

CONSULTANT:

We've successfully trained other government research scientists, even a whole department of Ph.D.'s. Our program is neither basic nor advanced—it's targeted to the individual. Since a person's work in the course builds from self-diagnosis of his or her on-the-job writing practices, we can meet a broad range of learning needs in the same room at the same time. The improvement goals people set for themselves determine whether, for the individual, the course is "basic" or "advanced."

HRD MANAGER:

I'm not sure how you pull that one off, but certainly those of your clients I've talked to confirm that you do. And all the other alternatives I've looked at sound pretty much like reruns of Freshman Composition. I'll propose to the economics department that we have you conduct a pilot workshop for them.

Scheduling the pilot workshop turned out to be more difficult than expected. The economists balked at even piloting, with a full group of participants, an unknown course. But they did name two people they were willing to send to assess a course if the HRD department ran it for a different group.

HRD MANAGER:

You said you could meet a broad range of needs in the same workshop, didn't you?

CONSULTANT:

That's right.

HRD MANAGER:

Then we'll go ahead and schedule a pilot course for the two economists to attend, and we'll fill out the enrollment with people from other departments. . . . Incidentally, I'm a bit concerned about Charles, one of the two economists designated to evaluate the program. He's known in the department as a traditionalist. William, on the other hand, is a relatively upbeat guy. He'll probably come to the course with an open mind.

Subsequently the workshop was attended by the two economists, a handful of other professionals from scattered departments of the agency, and several clerical employees who had been recruited at the last minute to fill the remaining seats. It achieved rave reviews from everyone except Charles, who (prodded by a Profession Bogey) cautiously suggested that, "CleaR is an interesting concept, but I'm not sure it is an appropriate style for professional economists to write." William, however, submitted a glowing assessment. "The CleaR style is exactly what we need to communicate with our large audience of noneconomists." So a spring workshop was booked, just for the economics department.

However, the HRD manager called with bad news less than two weeks before the course was scheduled to start.

HRD MANAGER:

No economists have signed up for the writing workshop. Their manager says their department hasn't yet decided whether to use your program. Given the assessments they got from the first course, they are still not sure it's suited to their special needs.

CONSULTANT:

But they got an enthusiastic recommendation from William, and only a mild hedge from Charles.

HRD MANAGER:

I know. But these are very careful people.

CONSULTANT:

So what are you going to do?

HRD MANAGER:

Rather than paying the late cancelation penalty, I want to go ahead and run the course. The pilot workshop was so popular that we've built up a long waiting list of people from other departments who've asked to attend. Given the short notice, not many professionals on the waiting list will be able to enroll. But as we did last time, we can fill the empty seats with clerical personnel.

CONSULTANT:

Fine. But what do you propose to do about the economists?

HRD MANAGER:

I've arranged for you to meet with senior members of the economics department while you're in town teaching the workshop. You can explain face-to-face how the program will meet their people's special needs.

The workshop was conducted, as was the session with senior management. As William had, they recognized that CleaR would precisely satisfy their intended objective of communicating economic concepts to lay audiences. So a third workshop was booked for the fall.

The HRD Manager again called less than two weeks before it was scheduled to start.

HRD MANAGER:

Bad news, I'm afraid. The economics department has refused to enroll anyone in your workshop. They've asked me to find them a more advanced program.

CONSULTANT:

A more advanced program?

HRD MANAGER:

That's right. Word got back to them that we've been running your workshop for the clerical staff. They say they obviously need a more advanced program than that.

The More Information Maze

The government economists were hiding in a familiar place: *We're not going to change our writing until we get exactly the right information on how to do it.* Then follows a search (which can last for years) for a special book or expert. To demonstrate the futility of hiding in the information maze, I want to tell a story of my own about Willoughby Johnson, a man who for over 40 years directed the composition program at the University of Missouri.

Professor Johnson turned youthful survivors of master's degree programs into instructors who taught the English department's 5,000 composition students—and thereby made a living during the four to eight years they spent getting a Ph.D. One of his favorite training devices for instructors was fondly known throughout the department as the "WJ note," mimeographed examples of which showed up regularly in all our mailboxes. It's been more than 30 years, but I can still remember the exact wording of some of them.

> I understand that certain instructors have been speaking harshly to their classes. Please keep in mind that some of your students are younger even than you.
>
> WJ

> It has come to my attention that some of you have announced to your students your disapproval of, and intention not to use, the textbook they have been required to purchase for Freshman Composition. I commend you on your initiative and independent judgment. Please leave a forwarding address with the secretary so she'll know where to send your final paycheck.
>
> WJ

This last WJ note has special relevance to our story. The book in question had been reapproved the previous year during a departmental meeting where several young instructors had querulously debated its merits versus those of a competing text. One faction wanted to adopt a new text whose author claimed his method was unique and more effective. The opposing group—who felt we were already using the best of

all possible methods for teaching writing—were as determined to retain the text we had been using.

A third group (to which I belonged, incidentally) agreed
with them, but for less high-minded reasons. Most of us
were half-time students (two graduate seminars per term)
as well as full-time teachers (four sections of composition).
We were raising families on less than laborers' incomes and,
between grading papers and jumping through the graduate
school's hoops, we were working 14-hour days, 7 days a
week. We just wanted to get our degrees and get out. The
last thing we needed was to redesign all our lesson plans to
fit a new textbook.

Willoughby Johnson, letting the argument continue until people started repeating themselves, intervened. "When
choosing a text for a composition course," he said, "the most
important thing to remember is that *none of them are any
good.*"

Will was correct. A well-written book on how to write is
considerably harder to find than a well-written book on how
to play tennis; and both, if read carefully, will have about
the same effect on one's game. People do not learn how to do
something better by reading the right book. Or by listening
to the right expert talk. They become better writers only *by
starting to write in different and more readable ways.*

The "As Soon As" Checklist

A search for a new book or a new guru are not the only reasons that can be given for postponing an attack on BoG. The
as soon as Hiding Places come in many other varieties too.
Please check all that apply.

We'll start writing better *as soon as:*

☐ We get everything else done.
☐ The revised manual comes out.

☐ We hire some new secretaries, ones that can spell.
☐ The new system comes on line.
☐ The reorganization is complete.
☐ Someone approves the workshop we recommended.
☐ Management agrees on what the guidelines should be.
☐ We find a time everyone can attend the meeting.
☐ More money gets allocated.
☐ We're not so busy.
☐ Lightning strikes our boss.
☐ All of the above

As any good officer knows, defending a fixed position too doggedly can be a serious mistake. The enemy can sneak up behind those who dig their trenches too deep. The following are war stories about two executives who were caught hiding from CleaR.

The Pros Who Still Don't Know What They Do for a Living

SHE:

We're not sure we really need something as involved as your workshop. Our staff are all professionals, and they can't spare the time for a two- or three-day course. We had something more like a half-day program in mind.

HE:

It's always hard to find time when everyone has a busy schedule. Tell me, what do you and your people do?

SHE:

Our job is to conduct various kinds of research studies for our clients. Technical feasibility, environmental impact, economics, that sort of thing.

HE:

So what do your clients get from you?

SHE:

I'm puzzled by your question, since you're a consultant your-self. They in effect get our expertise. Instead of having to hire specialists full-time, they access ours part-time. We do jobs for them that they don't have the technical capabilities to do for themselves.

HE:

I'm sure your people do excellent work, too. But what I won-dered was, what do your clients *get*? When they've paid your invoice, what do they have to show for it?

SHE:

Oh, well, we send them a report, of course.

HE:

In other words, IBM makes computers, Ford makes cars, and your company makes reports?

SHE:

Well, yes. I suppose you could put it that way.

HE:

What sort of quality control do you have for your reports?

SHE:

As I said, our people are all professionals. They knew how to write reports when we hired them.

HE:

So what did you have in mind when you contacted us? There must be some discomfort here about writing or you wouldn't have asked me to stop by.

SHE:

Well, our people don't all have the same opinions about how reports should be written. They feel they waste a lot of time when they have to collaborate on a report because they have different ideas about what's right. So we thought you might be able to give us a few guidelines about what's correct.

HE:

May I suggest that correctness is not the issue? That you should be concerned with effectiveness instead? You and your people should decide what impact you want your firm's reports to have. You should be looking at a report design and style that is a unique reflection of your professionalism and competence. Your clients ought to recognize, as soon as they start reading one of your reports, that it came from your company.

SHE:

Pardon me for laughing. We could never get our people to agree on any *one* way to write reports. They're too independent.

HE:

I'm certainly not talking about handcuffing anybody. But you can establish a set of organizing, style, and design practices within which everyone works. Then your reports would give an impression of consistent professionalism.

SHE:

When I try to visualize what you're suggesting, only one picture comes to mind . . . our people spending the next several months in meetings arguing their different points of view about report writing.

HE:

That's why we should get everyone together for two or three days. Then we can look at your reports from the reader's point of view. We can talk with each other about communications values and techniques rather than opinions. To replace the so-called rules everyone is citing, I'll show you some objective, modern criteria you can all use to manage writing. You'll be surprised, once everyone has the same tools, how easily they can work together solving writing problems. And you'll be pleased about how much more professional your reports become.

SHE:

Well, I don't know. We've got some exceptionally busy months ahead. In fact, we have nine major reports to do before the end of the year. Maybe after we've finished writing them we can take another look at your suggestion.

The chief consultant—a person who managed a firm that sold reports—tried to hide bad writing in the file labeled, *Minor problems we may get around to solving someday.* In the next story, the VP explains that he has hidden it in the file labeled, *Problems not important enough for people like me to bother with.*

The VP Explains Why Writing Isn't Important Enough to Manage

JOURNALIST:

Thanks for seeing me on such short notice.

VICE PRESIDENT:

We always look forward to visits from our friends from the press. So, I understand you're doing an article on business writing?

JOURNALIST:

Yes, and I'll explain the slant I'm working on. For years items have been showing up on the wire about some professor or other expert who's criticized business for its writing. I understand there have even been books written on the subject. The question I hope to answer in my article is, why doesn't somebody *do something* about the problem? Don't the people who run businesses care about bad writing?

VICE PRESIDENT:

Let me assure you first off that we care very much. We're always looking for new training programs and useful books and articles that can help our people write better. But these matters have to be put into perspective. Unlike you, we're not in the writing business. Running a corporation is a big and complicated job. People like me can't be going around making sure nobody dangles his modifier. (Hruph, ummph.)

JOURNALIST:

You seem to have quite a stack of paper on your desk.

VICE PRESIDENT:

Tell me about it! First thing every morning I have to start wading through the stuff that's piled up in my in-basket. In fact, I probably spend half my time reading. Most of these things are memos and reports from people in my division. That's how I keep track of what's going on in my area of responsibility and find out what initiatives we need to take.

JOURNALIST:

What's that document in the fancy cover?

VICE PRESIDENT:

Oh, that's a report I have to present to the board of directors next week. My people have been working on it for months. We need the board's approval for a major capital expenditure. (Incidentally, please don't say even that much in your article; our competitors would love to know that we're up to something.) Every time we want to launch a major project, we have to document our recommendations very carefully.

JOURNALIST:

It sounds to me as though writing is a pretty important activity in your company.

VICE PRESIDENT:

I suppose you might look at it that way. But you have to realize that most of our writing gets done at the lower levels in the organization.

JOURNALIST:

Could you give me an example?

VICE PRESIDENT:

Well, take this report for the Board, for instance. Some three or four dozen junior people conducted the studies that back it up. Then they did the actual writing when they produced their subreports. The department heads then just had to put all the subreports together and work them into a single submission on behalf of their department.

JOURNALIST:

And then?

VICE PRESIDENT:

The divisional managers formed a committee that combined all the departmental reports into a single document.

JOURNALIST:

So they're the ones who, in effect, produced the final version on your desk.

VICE PRESIDENT:

I wish they had! I did that version. It took me more than two weeks to go through the divisional manager's draft and clean it up for the Board. This is about half the length of what they sent me. And what a disjointed mess it was, too. I'm pretty proud of this thing.

JOURNALIST:

That sure seems like a lot of work . . . for you and everyone else involved.

VICE PRESIDENT:

People in business can't just go around shooting from the hip. Whenever we make a major decision anywhere in the company, we always have a written report or proposal in our hands. In fact, most of our professional staff spends 20 percent or more of their time writing memos and reports to management.

JOURNALIST:

People spend 20 percent of their time writing? That's not much less than I spend writing, and I make my living as a journalist. Let's see . . . a 40-hour week . . . 20 percent of that equals one fifth, or 8 hours. That's a full working day each week your people average writing. Would it be accurate, then, to say that of the total your company pays as salaries and benefits to its professionals, writing accounts for at least one fifth, or $1 of every $5?

VICE PRESIDENT:

Well . . . yes . . . I guess one could put it that way.

JOURNALIST:

All the office equipment I saw as I came in.... That looks like quite an investment too.

VICE PRESIDENT:

You better believe it! We've bought the latest word processing and copying equipment. And hired trained people to run it. You should see what we budget annually just for paper alone. We need good written communications, both internally with each other and externally with our dealers and customers.

JOURNALIST:

So what about this issue of persistent bad business writing?

VICE PRESIDENT:

As I said, it's all a matter of perspective. Now that you know more about how we operate, you'll understand why people like myself have to delegate the management of writing. That's the responsibility of people's immediate superiors. And they, in turn, can send people to the training department if they need help. Vice presidents shouldn't get involved in managing how the company turns out written documents.

Plenty of Places to Hide

There are many more places where people can hide from their Bogeys, and from the awareness that the organization is, every day, performing an important function in persistently bad ways, and from recognition that they are losing the Paper Wars. They can hide behind, for example, "Sure our writing's not great, but let me tell you who you should really be talking to." Or, "We don't have any choice; we're required to write the way we do." Or, "I won't do anything about the problem, but I'll tell someone else to." Or, "You just don't understand our unique situation."

As an alternative to hiding, people who prefer not to confront their Bogeymen can chase after Red Herrings instead. I'll address that topic in the next chapter. But first I want to tell you about the time Consultant explained *safe* writing to me.

Why CleaR Is the Safest Way to Write

Consultant was complaining. "When I propose that people write CleaR, they seem to think I'm trying to get them into trouble."

"Well you have to expect," I said, "that people who are accustomed to writing BoG will find CleaR pretty threatening. It's a major change."

"That's exactly the point! They don't recognize that *change* is what's scaring them, not CleaR itself. In a workshop or consulting session they'll compare the CleaR and BoG ways of writing sentences, of writing paragraphs and sections, of putting together whole documents. In every case, they will declare CleaR to be the more professional, informative, and easily read style. Then they will immediately start explaining why they can't or shouldn't write it—why they have to write BoG instead."

"If no one else writes that way, why should they risk it?"

"Other people *do* write that way. Every company and agency has its writers of CleaR, at every level. Often they are among the most effective and admired people in the organization because their writing projects decisiveness and clarity of thought. But others seem to feel safer imitating the mediocre than the exemplary."

"You have to admit that good writers have special talents."

"Everybody has special talents," Consultant replied. "And everyone needs to hone their communications abilities so they can demonstrate what their other talents are. Writing a good business or technical report is not like writing a great novel. People just have to use a few basic, common-sense techniques to write useful, readable business prose. Writing CleaR is easy. Giving up one's loyalty to BoG seems to be what's hard."

"But people often have pretty complicated information to deliver," I said. "And they have to give it just the right shade of meaning. Sometimes they can even be legally liable for what they say."

"All the more reason to write CleaR. A reader who has to sort out a complicated subject shouldn't have to struggle with complicated language as well. If people need to use technical terminology, they can still put their technical words in direct, readable sentences. And CleaR opens up a person's style for the expression of shades of meaning; BoG only obscures subtleties by making everything sound the same. As to the question of legal liability—if I ever have to defend a document in court, I want it to say exactly what I meant to say. I don't want it to contain ambiguous wording that a judge might interpret far differently. BoG simply isn't necessary. I have never—never in twenty years—found a BoG passage that could not be translated into CleaR . . . and made more understandable in the process."

"Still, I write CleaR because I'm a professional writer," I said. "But if I worked in government or industry, I think I might prefer to write BoG too."

"Why on earth would you want to do that?"

"Well, it just seems more impressive, somehow. More like what we used to read in textbooks. And it doesn't seem so . . . so confronting as CleaR. It would let me sort of skirt around issues rather than coming right out and saying things directly."

Consultant snorted. "BoG is indefensible! Although BoG writers sometimes go to great lengths to justify their style,

BoG serves no useful function. It is not impressive. It is not professional. It meets no legitimate standards of correctness or appropriateness. Complex ideas are not clarified by BoG; they are obscured by it. BoG does not soften unpleasant messages; it only attempts to hide them. People who hope BoG will somehow lend weight to *what* they write find their ideas discredited for *how* they write. In short, BoG is neither a style to be emulated nor a standard to be maintained. It is simply a bad habit sustained by precedent."

"I've never known you to be so eloquent," I said.

"It happens sometimes when somebody gets me stirred up."

CHAPTER 7

THE RED HERRINGS

Who can have the temerity to suggest that management's first responsibility is not to assure the writing turned out by the company is correct, acceptable, and appropriate?

The Smoked and Salted Fish

The Hiding Places discussed in the previous chapter are the reasons people give for not doing anything, or at least anything effective, to combat BoG. The Red Herrings we'll look at now are the safer enemies they choose to fight instead.

> **red her·ring,** *n.* A smoked and salted herring. A subterfuge whose object is to distract or divert notice from the relevant problem.

When Consultant started explaining the Red Herrings to me, I recognized immediately we were getting into my own area of expertise. The oldest and deepest Red Herrings in our minds—the really smoked and salted ones—are closely allied to what Consultant calls the School Bogeys. They are false scents that lead BoG hunters down dead-end trails, and they work so well because they seem so incontrovertible. Who, after all, can have the temerity to suggest that management's first and overriding responsibility regarding written communications is *not* to assure the writing turned out by the company is *correct, acceptable, and appropriate?*

So opportunities for victories are lost, and BoG prevails, when someone in power refuses to countenance an innovation because its proponents have not demonstrated that it is "correct" or "acceptable." And heaven help the underling who proposes a writing practice deemed to be "inappropriate."

These words have a powerful hold upon us. Therefore they are mighty Paper Wars weapons in the hands of those who wield them. But we should be suspicious. The very certitude of people who most readily use words like *incorrect* and *unacceptable* suggests that their case might be shaky. So let's do some serious thinking together about such words, adult to adult.

Correct and *Incorrect*

The concept behind *correct* seems simple enough. Something either conforms to established standards or it does not. So as we are writing, what are these "standards"? What criteria can we use to determine whether we are writing *correctly* or *incorrectly?*

Let's start with an easy topic—spelling. Supposedly when a word appears in a document its spelling can be judged either correct or incorrect, depending on whether it conforms to the dictionary model. But since dictionaries are compiled by people, we can appropriately raise a chicken-and-egg question: How did the people who wrote the dictionaries learn to spell?

Because English spelling has evolved in complicated ways and is governed by laws that are sometimes contradictory or inconsistently applied, it was for a long time very irregular and confused. Even Shakespeare (to use the currently accepted spelling) is known the have spelled his own name twelve different ways. In the 18th century, the kind of people who tend to such matters decided to bring order to lexicography, and they came to the quite reasonable conclusion that the spelling practices of people like themselves should provide the standard for everyone else. They looked at each appearance of a word in published documents written by people they considered to be appropriate models; then, in compiling their dictionaries, they spelled the word in the way it *most often* appeared in those documents. (They also defined each word according to what it usually *seemed* to mean in the various contexts provided by those documents.)

So in answering the question of how did the people who compiled the dictionaries learn to spell, we arrived at a sensible understanding—they generalized from the more frequent spelling practices of authors.

But let's see what happens if, in the process of thinking these things through together, we pose the question differently: How did the people who wrote the dictionaries learn to spell *correctly?* Now we have a question that cannot be answered without postulating some criteria totally different than the observed practices of established writers. If the word *correct* is added to the equation, spelling takes on overtones of the absolute and the eternal. Spelling no longer constitutes a reasonable agreement among ourselves to model our practices on those of our most skilled fellows. It becomes a matter of compliance, an obligation to conform to decreed standards or risk being exposed as one caught, not only red-handed but in black and white, making a mistake. There are those who seem to think that God and the dictionary are synonyms. (Just as there are those, I suspect, who wish Moses had thought to turn over the Tablets. They are sure the rules of English grammar, as well as the correct outline for a technical report, must have been chiseled into the back.)

Some might suggest that, as long as we instill the importance of good spelling in those who write our letters and reports, it little matters whether we choose to talk in terms of *correct/incorrect* or *standard/nonstandard.* But I think it matters very much, because the words affect how we relate to one another. They determine whether one person helps another communicate effectively, or simply punishes him for making mistakes. *Nonstandard* is an observation, *incorrect* an accusation. It is constructive (and generous) to assume a person who spells a word differently than the dictionary is unaware of the standard spelling. Lack of awareness is eas-

ily remedied. However, *incorrect* spelling is much more difficult to cure, rooted as it is in educational and perhaps even
intellectual shortcomings, not to mention the suspicion of
moral turpitude.

Those office terrorists who derive satisfaction from
searching out the spelling errors of others can be sanctimo-
nious and bad mannered, so we should all keep our dictionaries handy and try to keep our deficiencies hidden from
them. But we should never let anyone smoke screen BoG by
proclaiming spelling and grammar to be the battle ground
on which the Paper Wars are to be fought.

*   *   *   *   *

Thanks to the dictionaries, skirmishes over spelling result in quick and unambiguous victories. But the footing is
slippery for those who venture to lead a charge over the
mossy rocks known as *correct grammar.*

To begin with, the whole question of grammar is complicated by the reflection, in people's language, of their need
for social identification and differentiation. This is the force
that motivates many people to obey the grammatical laws of
their own group rather than the "standard English" perpetuated in schools and modeled in the media (except by some
sports broadcasters). The farmer who says *I seen* and *he
don't* is not necessarily ignorant of standard grammar; he
just wants to make sure nobody mistakes him for a city person. In some circles blacks have learned that "talking white"
can be punished by ostracism. And nine-year-old Johnny,
who continues to make the same grammatical errors in
spite of consistent and repeated correction (that is, nagging)
is demonstrating that at his age, boys are more concerned
with proving their linguistic loyalty to their buddies than to
their parents and teachers. Nor does Johnny eventually
"grow out of" his bad habits; he simply discovers, as he gets
older, that his best interests now lie in allying himself with
people who talk more like his parents did.

Like spelling standards, the "official" grammatical laws were derived, through observation and deduction, from the language behaviors of a defined population. But while spelling is modeled on one relatively identifiable population—those who write documents of sufficient merit to be printed—the grammatical models were drawn from the behaviors of a different population. The grammar we studied in school was supposedly based upon "educated usage." In fact, it was based on the formal, written usage of only the most educated. Even though generations of school children were drilled in that usage, they probably never heard it spoken except in the classroom, and then only during grammar lessons in English class. The finer points of that grammar are seldom observed in real life except in the conversation of a highly educated, language-sensitive minority.

The working language of today's corporate and governmental offices, both spoken and written, conforms to grammatical laws that are less precise and consistent than those of traditional, schoolroom grammar. These laws are based on a broader (but not more democratic) model—the language behaviors of white middle-class urbanites who have a general education.

Therefore, business documents will *always* be vulnerable to the attacks of grammatical purists. The form of English we all use daily is simply not the one that was once taught in the schools. So if we allow grammatical purity to be the standard by which writing is judged, we surrender the Paper Wars to the faultfinders who champion caution at the expense of communication.

*   *   *   *   *

So where, in all these layers of Paper Wars criteria, does the idea of *correct* fit? Nowhere, as nearly as I can tell. Consultant says the longer he teaches writing the fewer uses he finds for the word. One time, for instance, while consulting with a young woman who spoke fluent "white office English," he was able to explain certain grammatical problems in her letters and memos as intrusive fragments of the "black street English" she spoke after hours. He thinks the explanation helped her. He doubts that red-penciling her "grammatical errors" would have been nearly as constructive.

* * * * *

Having followed some flights of fancy, and having toyed with arguments that might tempt the argumentative to propose the patently absurd conclusion that there are no such things as errors of spelling and grammar, let's grant that standards do exist, and let's acknowledge that adhering to them is a good thing to do. But let's also recognize that words like *correct* and *incorrect* are not insightful terms that can help us build better ways of communicating; they are simply blunt instruments that can be used only to end (not necessarily win) skirmishes in the Paper Wars. And to the extent that they distract us from the real battle, the one against BoG, they are but Red Herrings dragged, smelling, across the trail.

Acceptable and *Unacceptable*

The Red Herring issue is not nearly as complicated when we consider the words *acceptable* and *unacceptable*. Used by the uninformed to perpetuate the unreasonable, they are simply the cheap shots of the Paper Wars. Whatever is presently done is, obviously, *acceptable;* and anything new, because it is not being done, is automatically suspect of being *unacceptable*.

Incorrect at least suggests that one's writing is being judged according to some established standard. But *unacceptable* carries connotations of the subjective and the spur-of-the-moment—the kind of word a teacher once might have used to rule on a writing practice she did not like, but for reasons she could not explain.

Consultant says he's never comfortable even answering "yes" when someone asks, "Is this acceptable?"

Appropriate and *Inappropriate*

Now to the two big-bang words, *appropriate* and *inappropriate*. All discussion ends when someone in authority rules that a certain practice is *not appropriate* to business or technical writing.

I remember being taught in school that there were three "levels" of writing—formal, informal, and colloquial—and that certain practices were *appropriate* and *inappropriate* to each. The school paper that was mimeographed every Friday, with its liberal use of !!!, ???, (Teehee), and (Smile), provided a good example of the *colloquial,* a type of writing that clearly had specialized uses. The *formal* level was best illustrated, we were told, by "sermons, graduation speeches, and such." To the best of my memory, it was characterized by the presence of something called "formal expressions," and by the absence of such shortcuts as contractions. Everything that was neither distinctively colloquial nor formal belonged in the broad, multipurpose category labeled *informal.*

Now, even after more than a quarter of a century of professional involvement with written communications, I'm not sure I can consistently distinguish between "formal" and "informal" writing, or that I can always prescribe what is appropriate to one and not to the other.

But Consultant regularly meets executives, lit and alit, who work under no such disadvantage. They can detect with absolute certainty which writing practices are and which are not *appropriate* to their organization, which create a "proper, businesslike impression" or are suitable for a "formal technical report." And they are especially acute about zeroing in on those practices which they consider "too informal." When given a choice between the direct, easily read sentences of CleaR and the indirect, wordy sentences of

Bog, these executives are likely to pronounce BoG "more appropriate to our kind of writing." Somehow the schools' superficial and vague efforts to explain "formal expression" have been translated into mandated imprecision. A person should, it seems, avoid being *too* clear when writing about serious and important matters.

Consultant once tried to analyze his obvious lack of understanding regarding this need, so apparent to others, to write BoG. Perhaps he was missing some important part of the equation. So he searched his memory for the most important, most serious, most technical document his clients had ever asked him to look at. If he analyzed it carefully, perhaps he would discover why such documents are most appropriately written in the indirect, wordy manner of BoG.

Selecting the document was easy. A major defense contractor had recently asked for his help with a twelve-volume sales proposal. Consultant is constrained by professional ethics (and national security laws) from disclosing any details. But the document clearly qualified as important. He said he could tell that immediately when he saw the price quotation: in the neighborhood of $800 million. As well, the seller and the buyer both seemed to be very serious and businesslike about the matter, as well they should be when national defense is at stake. And the proposal definitely had to be considered technical, involving as it did a purposeful bringing together of radar, computers, guns, rockets, and high-performance jet aircraft.

The more Consultant thought about that proposal—about what kinds of people had written it, and why; about what kinds of people would read it, and why—the more convinced he became that such documents *have to be written in clear, simple language.* They are too expensive to produce; they play too large a part in the success, even survival, of the organizations that create them; they have too great an impact on the work effectiveness of the people who have to read and act upon them; in short, they are *too important and too serious* to write in BoG.

The organizations that have to write such documents cannot afford to let them become complicated and confusing monuments to the phobias of those least comfortable with written expression. In the context of winning or losing multimillion dollar contracts, disdaining clarity in favor of some vague, self-protective notion of appropriateness is silly and pedantic. Self-destructive, even.

The only *appropriate* writing is that which has the intended effect upon the intended reader. No one wants to buy something they are confused about, and no one wants to cooperate with a person who seems to take pains to restrict the amount of information that gets communicated. On the other hand, no one—regardless of how highly educated or highly promoted they are—is offended by a clearly written document that can be read quickly, easily, and with full understanding. People often explain that they "have to" use abstract, complicated language. But they find Consultant quarrelsome on the subject. Having failed to figure out why BoG would be appropriate in an $800 million proposal, he's not sensitive to its special propriety in an $80 letter.

Smoking Out the Red Herrings

The Red Herrings of *correctness, acceptability,* and *appropriateness* are not matters that should seriously concern business and technical writers or those who manage them. Except for the fact that, between the chaos of English lexicography and the allure of television—few of us (me included) can consistently depend upon our spelling—hardly any significant problems with "correct" English are to be found in the mainstream of business writing. (Certainly some younger or educationally disadvantaged employees are functional illiterates, or close to it; but that's a much different problem organizations have to solve.) Moreover, the few errors that do turn up with any regularity in business writing are *caused,* not prevented, by BoG.

Certainly a purist can always find things to mark. Dangling modifiers, for instance, are a persistent feature of business, and especially technical, writing. They may be inelegant, but most alits can't see them and few lits care. Much the same is true regarding other so-called errors. Despite the many times our English teachers explained the difference between *shall* and *will,* few of us ever use *shall.* Nor should we. For decades it's been nothing but an affectation (even in legal writing) for all but a very small portion of the population. Energies can be expended debating *like* versus *as, different from* versus *different than, who* versus *whom;* but much more important writing issues await our attention. Most writers of CleaR—provided they're careful to check their spelling, and provided they don't have a closet English teacher lurking somewhere on the premises—simply do not have to worry about making errors of English that matter.

Writers of BoG, on the other hand, are continually in danger of making three specific grammatical errors. Because BoG requires the use of so many nouns that have no meaning, writers can easily lose track of which hook they hung their sentence on. So failures of subject-verb agreement occur:

> One *aspect* of the many problems associated with the production of spare parts *are....*

> The *extent* of the differences between the original specifications and the new ones *are....*

For the same reason, BoG makes it unnecessarily difficult to keep nouns and pronouns sorted out:

> The coordination of the program for employee development will require modification of the existing policies that have been instituted in order to achieve compliance with laws assuring employment opportunities of members of minority groups. This means that....

(Consultant has heard of a manager who, when he heard that the nouns and pronouns sometimes didn't agree in the writing of his employees, solved the problem by forbidding his people to use pronouns.)

Breakdowns in parallelism are the third common problem in BoG. BoG sentences are unnecessarily complicated because they carry so much of their meaning in elaborate strings of prepositional phrases and intruded clauses. Few people have the syntactical skills needed to consistently keep everything lined up and dovetailed—parallel, in other words. (Another manager, listening to Consultant's explanation of how BoG strings together prepositional phrases, once asked, "Are you saying that we should avoid using prepositions?")

Thus BoG is the cause, not the cure, of the few instances of "incorrect grammar" that turn up with any consistency in business writing. Even so, BoG should be replaced primarily because it makes reading difficult and clouds understanding, not because it invites certain grammatical errors.

There are other Red Herrings besides correctness, acceptability, and appropriateness. Just as the word *might* can give away a Bogey, *supposed to* is the signal identifying the Roseate Fish:

I always thought you were supposed to start a letter with. . . .

Our last instructor said we were never supposed to. . . .

I assume you're going to tell people how they're supposed to write a. . . .

At the beginning of this chapter a Red Herring was defined as "a subterfuge whose object is to distract or divert notice from the relevant problem." The ones we have looked at are so enduring because they are so effective. They've assured that several generations of managers have run right past BoG and gone chasing off on false trails. One of the most dependable strategies of BoG defenders is to insist some other problem be solved instead.

The very first step executives must be prepared to take, in order to win the Paper Wars, is the wholehearted abandonment of BoG and its allied Red Herrings. Corporate energies must be turned to looking for reasons to *change* rather than rationalizations for remaining the same. Those reasons are close at hand—our Inner Readers have been whispering them in our ears for years.

CHAPTER 8

THE FRUITS OF VICTORY

*The writing in a reader-focused
organization is, above all, helpful.*

Telling Who's Won

"How can you tell?" I asked.

"What?"

"How can you tell when an organization has won the Paper Wars? When it has kicked out its Bogeys and put management's Inner Readers in charge of written communications? How does its writing differ?"

"Oh, the differences are vast," Consultant answered. "To begin with, the writing in a reader-focused organization is *purposeful*. Or to put it another way, *helpful*. Every document shows it was written with an unwavering sense of what job the writer wants to help the reader do, or of what understanding the writer intends to help the reader achieve. You can tell immediately writers know that providing others with clear, efficient help is their sole reason for writing, and that the corporate culture has succeeded in giving them permission to do the job in direct, communicative ways.

"One of the fringe benefits of managing an organization that has won the Paper Wars," Consultant went on, "is that less gets written. In an environment where documents are understood to be tools people write in order to achieve specific work goals, fewer vague, protective just-in-case documents get circulated for the files. As well, confident documents that are built from an early and explicit purpose statement are usually 40 percent to 60 percent shorter than timorous ones that try to construct a case first, then declare a purpose."

"You keep insisting that those who win the Paper Wars start doing just a *few* things well," I said. "Can you list them?"

"Sure," Consultant answered. He named the five winning practices that produce CleaR, the alternative to BoG:

1. CleaR is deductive writing. That is, it makes statements, then supports them with proof.
2. CleaR presents information instead of mere facts.
3. CleaR talks about people and things instead of ideas.
4. CleaR uses sentences with strong sentence cores.
5. And CleaR deals constructively with feelings.

Consultant went on to explain what he meant by each.

Deductive Writing—What Readers Want to Read

Inductive thinking makes strong science. *Inductive writing* makes weak communications. Certainly conclusions, to be sound, must be derived inductively from open-minded consideration of all the data. But once formulated, those conclusions—if they are to be communicated clearly and efficiently to another person—must be presented *deductively*. That is, they must first be stated, then they must be single-mindedly explained using only selected data that demonstrates their accuracy.

Consultant insists that becoming a *deductive* presenter of information is the single most powerful change a person—

or an organization—can make in communications technique, whether written or oral. The person who habitually makes statements, then explains them, projects an impression of being informed, professional, decisive, even fair and honest, and understandable.

Inductive Writing (BoG)

We interviewed several people who were in or around the pool at the time of the accident, but they all said they did not notice the victim enter the water. When we talked with the victim's friends, they reported that they were seated in deck chairs facing away from the pool. Even the pool manager could say only that the victim and his friends seemed to be "quiet and orderly." Therefore we have been unable to locate an eyewitness.

Deductive Writing (CleaR)

We could not locate an eyewitness who saw the victim enter the water. His friends said they were seated in deck chairs facing away from the pool, and none of the other patrons we interviewed happened to notice him. Even the pool manager could only say that the victim and his friends were "quiet and orderly."

Making Information Out of Facts

CleaR is an *interpretive* way of writing that turns mere facts into information. It cites only the most relevant data, and it expresses them in ways that reveal their significance.

People who have learned to write deductively are well on their way to writing interpretively as well. But they need to be sure they make explicit statements. The whole point is to tell people what we mean—not to tell them something else and hope they figure out what we are getting at. Some examples of interpretive and noninterpretive writing are shown below.

Noninterpretive	Interpretive
We should purchase the A–57 drive.	We should purchase the *large capacity* A–57 drive.
The second test produced a difference in speed of +11.5 seconds.	The speed on the second test *improved* by 11.5 seconds.
Daily production averaged 374 units last year and 408 units this year.	Since last year, average daily production *has increased* from 374 units to 408 units.
The heat increased the pressure in the line and the seals burst.	The seals burst *because* the heat increased the pressure in the line.

Writing about People and Things

Organizations are groups of people, located in places, working together, usually with the help of things. Does the old school definition come to mind? "A *noun* is a word that names a person, place, or thing." Unfortunately, the old definition is incomplete. The category noun also includes such words derived from verbs as *utilization, optimization,* and *finalization;* such words derived from modifiers as *effectiveness, viability,* and *consistency;* and such meaningless abstractions as *aspect, indication,* and *situation.* None of these words, by any stretch of the imagination, name people or things (or places)—instead, they are attempts to name concepts. Yet the BoG style uses them consistently in trying to communicate about people and things, and about what they are doing.

CleaR is so effective at communicating what *is*—or *could, should,* or *might* be—happening within organizations because it uses nouns that name people and things rather than nouns intended to communicate concepts. Here are some examples.

BoG	CleaR
The appropriate time for her to make her decision will not be until after the meeting.	She should not decide until after the meeting.
The results of the directive were not of an order that could be measured.	The directive produced no measurable results.
A necessary requirement for the functioning of the pipeline at full capacity is that all pumps must be in operation.	Unless all the pumps are operating, the pipeline will not carry its full capacity.
Our willingness to participate would be dependent upon their requesting our assistance.	If they asked us to participate, we would.

By focusing on people and things, CleaR also focuses on *actors,* and therefore upon *actions.* Organizations exist solely because of what they *do.* And written communications play a major role in helping management decide what to do, then to give directions for getting it done. Yet when we read documents written in BoG we get the impression that nothing ever happens—and if something does happen, nobody did it.

Francis Bacon once defined style as "the right words in the right places." That explanation starts to make sense when one considers the important difference between the kind of words CleaR and BoG put in the "noun places." When people complain about the "big words" used in BoG they are not so much talking about technical terms (which are often necessary, and can be defined), but what Consultant calls "zero" words (*practicability* and *substantiation,* for example). These are words that have almost no inherent communication value of their own—they acquire meaning only from the context in which they are used. Thus the writer of BoG starts with zero words, then tries to add enough modifiers and prepositional phrases to give the zero words some weight.

The writer of CleaR, on the other hand, communicates with a reader by creating mental pictures from nouns that name people and things, then fills in the picture with verbs that tell what the people and things are doing and modifiers that tell what they are like.

Using Strong Sentence Cores

The BoG writing style is not a word problem only. It is even more a sentence problem. BoG and CleaR use the sentence core in much different ways.

At the core of every sentence or clause there is a subject, a verb, and usually an object or complement:

- The audit *supervisor wrote* a complimentary *report* about their department.
- According to the forecast, the fourth *quarter looks promising*.
- After *we revised* the installation *specifications* for the plant, the *contractors* all *submitted* new *proposals*.

Writers of CleaR use this subject-verb-object/complement core to state the primary information carried by a sentence. In fact, the cores of CleaR sentences can usually stand alone as complete statements that make sense: *The supervisor wrote a report; we revised the specifications; the contractors submitted proposals.* With the primary information standing firmly in the sentence core, writers can express all secondary information by attaching adjectives and prepositional phrases to that core.

Writers of BoG, on the other hand, say almost nothing in the core of the sentence: *appropriate time will not be until; results were not of an order; requirement is; willingness would be dependent upon.* Having used up their cores saying nothing, BoG writers are left with only the adjective and prepositional phrase positions to carry all the information, primary and secondary, the sentence is intended to communicate.

Weak-Cored BoG Sentences	Strong-Cored CleaR Sentences
A failure of the shaft would mean that the replacement of the whole unit would be necessary.	If the shaft failed, the whole unit would have to be replaced.
An attempt to utilize the program would create insurmountable problems for them.	They would not be able to make the program work.
Our willingness to participate would be dependent upon their requesting our assistance.	If they asked us to participate, we would.

People complain about BoG's long sentences as well as its big words. Again, the problem is not what it at first seems. Readers can track long sentences—if those sentences are cleanly constructed and punctuated. But they have difficulty tracking the excessive number of *function* words in BoG sentences (prepositions like *of, for,* and *from*—articles like *the* and *a*). Because BoG sentences are built from empty cores, they have to cram most of their information into long strings of prepositional phrases. The little words needed to build these phrases carry no information for the reader—their job is to make the mess stick together. Yet the reader's mind has to process each of them, puzzling out what connects with what, in order to determine what the sentence "probably means."

BoG not only uses the sentence core to carry *little* information; it often uses it to carry the *wrong* information. For example, writers of BoG habitually try to make the core do the work of communicating qualifications, when other parts of the sentence can do that job much better:

How BoG Qualifies	*How CleaR Qualifies*
It is possible that they will adopt the program.	They *may* adopt the program.
It is evident that our manager thinks the *probability* of their adopting the program *is* relatively *high*.	Our manager *seems* to think they will *probably* adopt the program.
It is certain that the figures are correct. However, at this point in time the *accuracy* of the interpretation *is questionable*.	We are *sure* the figures are correct, but we *do not yet* know *whether* we have interpreted them accurately.

The BoG style also tries to use the sentence core to make connections that are best left to words especially intended for that task:

BoG Connections	*CleaR Connections*
The *reason* she fired him *was because of* his incompetence.	She fired him *because* he was incompetent.
A necessary *requirement* for the functioning of the pipeline at full capacity *is that* all pumps must be in operation.	*Unless* all the pumps are operating, the pipeline *will not* carry its full capacity.

The subject-verb-object/complement core is the part of the sentence that can transport by far the heaviest load of meaning. Therefore CleaR uses it to do the sentence's primary job, expressing the major idea. Then the subordinate words—adjectives, adverbs, prepositional phrases, auxiliary verbs, conjunctions—can do their lesser work of communicating attributes, qualifications, connections, and shades of meaning.

Being Human about Feelings

"Now, about feelings," I proposed.

"Ah yes. Feelings," Consultant sighed. "May I quote somebody?"

"Be my guest. I'll write down whatever you say."

"Well, then." He assumed a portly stance. "We have nothing to fear but fear itself."

"An appropriately war-like quote," I said.

"People seem so fearful about writing," Consultant said, "even though 90 percent of organizational writing deals with ho-hum, business-as-usual issues. They seem to think that everything they write is likely to anger someone. And when the topic or purpose of the document actually *will* hurt or anger someone, they get even more tongue-tied. They intensify the reader's emotional response by trying to ignore or avoid it."

"So what do you propose?" I asked.

"Strong feelings—either in ourselves or in other people—are always difficult to deal with," he answered. "But learning to manage and communicate in emotional situations requires adult skills we all have to learn at some point. Those same skills are as applicable when writing as they are when speaking face-to-face with an upset person, or when bringing bad news.

"First of all," he said, "we must acknowledge what the other person is feeling. So rather than, for instance, starting off a bad news letter by pretending it's a good news letter, we should begin with an announcement of the bad news, coupled with a statement recognizing that the recipient will not feel good about it."

"Could you give me an example or two?" I asked.

"How about, *'We're sorry to have to inform you . . .,* or, *I know you will be disappointed to hear. . . .*

"Okay," I said, "then what?"

"Then, after announcing the bad news, we should say what we can to make the reader feel more positive. If there is hope, we should offer it. *Perhaps we can make some other arrangements.* Or, *Although we can't help you, I suggest you contact. . . .* If there is no hope, we can at least offer them encouragement and affirmation. *We have valued the work you have done for us.* Or, *I hope your next position proves to be more successful.*"

"What if I don't like the jerk?" I asked. "Do I get to tell him off?"

"Only if you want to get fired," Consultant snorted. "You should use writing as a means of helping your reader, not as a way of venting your own emotions. Angry or destructive words have no place in business writing—ever. The predictable result of anger is anger. And neither our anger nor another person's can serve any constructive ends.

"Besides," he said, "if you really want to sock it to someone, just write bad news in the distant, impersonal tone traditionally used in business writing. That can send a chill down a reader's spine.

"The writer's job is to *affect* the reader in *predictable* and *constructive* ways, and that applies to affecting his or her feelings as well as understanding. A few well-chosen and well-placed positive words can create very constructive effects in a letter or memo. When it comes to writing as one human to another, a little good sense goes a long way."

Getting It All Sorted Out

"So let's sum up," I proposed. "People—and organizations—who want to write well should, first of all, start writing deductively."

Consultant nodded.

"And they should write interpretively."

Consultant nodded again.

"And they should write in the CleaR style by using nouns that actually name people and things, and by writing full rather than empty sentence cores. In other words, they should never use BoG sentences that have empty cores built from zero words."

"I didn't say that," Consultant answered.

"Didn't say what?"

"I didn't say people should *never* use BoG sentences."

"But . . . that's what you've had me leading up to since we started on this project! Our whole purpose has been to demonstrate that BoG is wrong."

"Where'd you ever get a silly idea like that?" he said. "BoG sentences, like all the rest, have their uses. They can, if used sparingly, help us make emphatic statements like, *It is important to remember . . .* , or *The service aspect must be emphasized.* They can, if used sparingly, help us state abstract principles like *Implementation of the program might be difficult,* or *Accountability is the key to assuring training effectiveness.* And BoG sentences can be used, sparingly, to add occasional variety in our sentence rhythms. The problem is not that people write a BoG sentence now and then.

It's that they write BoG sentences too consistently; that they try to make BoG do too many jobs it can't do. Good style is a matter of proportion, not avoidance."

"Okay," I recanted. "Writers should write a style containing a high proportion of CleaR sentences that build full cores from concrete nouns; and they should use the weaker BoG cores and zero words sparingly, but to achieve specific effects."

"That's better," Consultant said.

"And they should write like human beings."

"By George, I think you've got it!"

"So now all they have to do is figure out *how* to write the way you describe."

"Sometimes I wonder why I ever picked you for this job."

"What have I done wrong this time?"

"They already know how to write well, dummy. That's what we were saying when I had you explain about the Inner Writer and the Inner Reader, about the warehouse and the Bogeys and the keys, and about making choices and getting involved and changing things. You may have clarified some technical points here and there, but you haven't told people anything about good writing that, deep down, they don't already know. Your job isn't to tell them how to write well; you're just here to tell them it's okay to go ahead and start doing it."

CHAPTER 9

THE FALSE ALLIES AND LOSING STRATEGIES

Why do organizations return,
year after year, to solutions
that have proven not to work?

Things Either Change, or They Don't

"The main reason executives can't win the Paper Wars," Consultant proclaimed, "is because they remain loyal to old allies and strategies that consistently betray them."

I don't have to tell you, by now, how uncompromising Consultant can be. He insists that I impress upon you a startling—but apparently unavoidable—conclusion: Whatever methods you may currently be using to fight the Paper Wars, those methods are *not working* unless they are producing immediate and dramatic improvements in your organization's writing.

Here's how he put it. "Executives typically attack written communications problems with one of, or a combination of, three methods: manager editing, written guidelines or statements of policy, and training programs (conducted either by internal or external workshop leaders). Yet in spite of these three solutions, and in spite of their persistent use for perhaps years, the writing problems remain. BoG continues to be the reigning form of written communications, and the Paper Wars go on without respite.

"Management has to respond to the obvious. No rationalizations can hide the fact that any solution that doesn't work is *not* a solution. If we look at the *non*-results of the familiar, traditional forms of editing, legislating, and train- ing, we can come to only one of two conclusions: They either leave BoG unaffected, or they in fact encourage its use."

Consultant is essentially correct, however much a per- son might wish him a trifle less dogmatic. One of the more puzzling aspects of the Paper Wars is why organizations try to solve the problem of bad written communications by re- turning, year after year, to solutions that have proven not to work. BoG, with all its attendant costs and frustrations, persists; yet so do the established responses to it.

Now that Consultant has opened that can of worms, we should look carefully at what *actually* happens when the traditional methods are attempted. First to the conventional internal solutions, manager editing, legislating, and train- ing conducted by the in-house staff.

The Old Standbys: Editing, Legislating, Internal Training

Few practices are more expensive or pointless than having a highly paid executive trying to teach subordinates how to write by spending hours editing the documents they submit. Yet manager editing is the single solution most often cited in response to the question, "What are you presently doing to improve people's writing?"

Consultant has serious reservations about "correction" as a teaching tool, even in the hands of those, such as En- glish teachers, who might be expected to be skilled in using it. For one thing, it lacks system. People learn from feedback by putting individual datum into general thought patterns that shape interpretation and memory. But what conclu- sions can an employee (or a student) draw from the dispar- ate combination of error labeling, word substitution, and sentence rewriting that marks up the returned report (or school essay)? What conclusions, that is, beyond the obvious one—that he or she has screwed up again?

People have told Consultant some of the things they've "learned" by trying to generalize from the written comments of teachers and superiors. "Every paragraph is supposed to be five sentences long." (Honest to gosh. Someone actually said that.) "We're not supposed to use the word _____." (You can insert just about any entry in *Webster's*.) "We can't begin a sentence with the word _____." (Ditto.) "Whenever we write a report, we always have to. . . ." "All our letters must begin with. . . ." "I can't do that. My boss never allows it." "Oh, no, you don't. I tried that once and got stomped on."

So the editing typically done by managers, in addition to being a wasteful way for the boss to spend time, is just another means used to perpetuate the notion that writing is an act of self-defense. Even worse, the most predictable outcome of manager editing seems to be *more* manager editing. People frequently admit to growing careless about their writing: "Why bother to knock myself out? My boss just changes everything I write anyway." The manager who edits a lot, and who also has the impression that people's writing seems to be getting worse, might well ponder the Law of Unintended Consequences.

The second traditional way of tackling the writing problem is legislating—that is, the compilation of "writing guidelines" or "style manuals" that decree which Red Herrings are to be observed, and which Bogeys are perceived the most sensitive, in the particular organization. Legislating is no more likely than editing to produce improvements. To begin with, guidelines almost always end up focusing on cosmetic issues, like how letters should be formatted and what euphemisms are officially approved. But even those that deal with substantive issues have little effect. After all the meetings, after all the heated discussions and painful compromises, after the guidelines are finally written up, proofed, printed, bound, and distributed, such documents quickly work their way to the bottoms of drawers, or to the ends of bookshelves, rarely to be seen again. Their contents will be remembered only by a few Paper Wars combatants who have discovered that, dug out and dusted off, they can be used in winning arguments—usually about which forms of CleaR are not allowed.

As to the value of internal training in combating BoG, heaven help the lowly HRD staffer who dares to challenge some manager's favorite practices. As he or she will soon be informed, the purpose of a writing course is to teach the established and accepted, not the new and more effective.

In short, the main reason that editing doesn't work, and legislating doesn't work, and having the training staff develop a course doesn't work, is that the forces protecting BoG try to co-opt *any* internal measures and turn them to their own ends. All three methods are among the organization's most powerful means of propagating its Bogeys and of teaching people which forms of BoG are most propitious.

The standard external solution—bringing in an outside expert—often fails for the same sorts of reasons. In selecting an outsider, management is likely to use criteria that assure BoG remains unthreatened, as the following war story illustrates.

The Client Who Wanted More BoG, Not Less

HRD DIRECTOR:

Our executives are complaining that the reports their employees are writing aren't very helpful. They don't give enough information.

CONSULTANT:

What kind of information are your executives asking for?

HRD DIRECTOR:

They say they get reports that just consist of tables of data and a few bare statements about them. They don't know how they're supposed to interpret the information in the tables.

CONSULTANT:

Sure, that's a common problem. Younger employees need to learn how to build a case. They don't yet know how to interpret and organize data to create information that management can use in making decisions. Those are skills we teach as a regular part of our workshops.

HRD DIRECTOR:

How then do you explain this? (*He held up the page in the pamphlet Consultant had given him that illustrated the style differences between BoG and CleaR.*)

CONSULTANT:

I don't understand what you mean.

HRD DIRECTOR:

(*He pointed to the examples of the CleaR writing style, which is less wordy than the BoG style.*) This suggests that your writing course, like most others, tries to get people to use fewer words.

CONSULTANT:

Well, we certainly don't think readers should have to process more words than they need.

HRD DIRECTOR:

But I told you that we want our people to provide *more* information, *not less.* We don't want someone to come in and teach them to write shorter reports. Their reports are too short already.

Consultant took the bait. He thought he had encountered an alit who failed to grasp the fact that the volume of information communicated is distinctly different than the volume of words used in communicating it. He launched into a "lecturette" on how, in fact, writers who use fewer words not only communicate information more efficiently, but they "leave themselves room" to communicate even more information. Those who write in the BoG style can delude themselves into thinking they are saying something simply because they are filling space.

The HRD Director was not convinced, of course. Mumbling, "I realize now that perhaps we need to give more thought to what we want the program to achieve," he ushered Consultant to the door with a promise to contact him "when our plans are firmed up." He then picked up the phone and hired one of Consultant's English teacherly competitors.

Later Consultant discovered what he should have researched before he went in—that the company he was approaching had a reputation as being among the most careful and conservative in the industry. He hadn't simply given the HRD Director the wrong answer, he had scared the daylights out of him and had set his Bogeys to buzzing. When the Director compared BoG and CleaR, he recognized that the traditional BoG was what his managers wanted. He had been assigned to assure they got more of it, not less.

Good Help Is Tough to Find Nowadays

It is definitely not easy for the modern executive, faced with making a serious and costly decision, to determine the best outside expert to hire to help fight BoG. Sorting out your own expectations, the candidate's paper credentials, and the candidate's claims about the unique virtues of his or her methodology can complicate the decision to the point of paralysis.

Asking about degrees doesn't help. Universities grant degrees in English literature or in English education; but they do not train people to teach their fellow working adults how to write more professionally.

And even checking references may not guarantee a good decision. The people you are invited to contact are likely to praise the trainer for getting good course evaluations. But *all workshop leaders get good course evaluations.* As a minimum job competency, trainers must be able to teach a course in a manner that assures people leave feeling good about having attended it. Those who cannot accomplish that basic task with some consistency are quickly weeded out of the profession. You're not interested in whether people liked the trainer; you want to find out whether people quit writing BoG, and started writing CleaR, as a result of the instruction. But the previous clients probably didn't ask that question themselves.

Little wonder then, when approving the selection of a consultant to lead an attack on BoG, managers are likely to choose the one who promises to do what their favorite English teacher did, or who claims to do the job fastest and for the least amount of money, or who seems the least likely to stir up the local Bogeys. Moreover, as the following story demonstrates, it's too easy to expect too little.

The Company Hires Some High-Priced Help

Consultant recognized, as soon as the meeting opened, where the Divisional Manager was hiding the company's BoG—in the file labeled *Problems we've already solved.*

DIVISIONAL MANAGER:

Thank you for asking, but n⌐, we don't have any problems with writing.

CONSULTANT:

What an unusual company!

DIVISIONAL MANAGER:

Oh, we used to, certainly. But we've taken care of them.

CONSULTANT:

What did you do?

DIVISIONAL MANAGER:

We have been using some people who teach Business English at the community college. Very competent they are too. They all have Master's degrees, and one even has a Ph.D.

CONSULTANT:

What do they do for you?

DIVISIONAL MANAGER:

They've been running writing courses for our people. For over three years now, in fact. The training department is very pleased. They say the writing workshops produce some of the best course evaluations of any programs we offer.

CONSULTANT:

So what changes have you seen in people's writing since you started using the program?

DIVISIONAL MANAGER:

Changes?

CONSULTANT:

Yes. What improvements have you seen in the letters and reports people are writing?

DIVISIONAL MANAGER:

Oh, well, I don't suppose we really expected any big changes. These things take time, you know.

CONSULTANT:

You must have invested quite a bit in the program.

DIVISIONAL MANAGER:

We sure have. Experts aren't cheap, as I'm sure you're aware. But it's worth it. When we bring in someone who really knows what they're talking about, it shows our people that we're serious about helping them improve their performance.

CONSULTANT:

What performance improvements are the writing courses producing?

DIVISIONAL MANAGER:

Well, this isn't really my line of work, as you'll understand. In fact, being a specialist in writing yourself, you'd probably be able to explain better than I can what we're getting.

CONSULTANT:

Indeed I might. But I'm not authorizing payment of the invoices or approving people's being away to attend the courses. If you don't mind telling me, I am curious to know what you see your company as getting for your investment.

DIVISIONAL MANAGER:

Well, I suppose that, besides making our people feel well taken care of, the program is teaching them how to write correct and acceptable letters and reports.

CONSULTANT:

Oh. Correct and acceptable.

DIVISIONAL MANAGER:

That's right. If anybody understands how important that is, you should.

CONSULTANT:

Yes, I understand about correct and acceptable.

English Teachers Make Poor Allies

One of the easiest mistakes to make, when looking for help with writing problems, is to hire an English teacher. Who better suited, we think, to be an expert on writing?

But the truth is that most of what English teachers teach, writers do not need to know. Only other English teachers need to know it. And even if writers do know it, that knowledge has little effect upon their performance as they sit, pen in hand or fingers on the keyboard, writing.

Yet people continue to be convinced their writing suffers either because they still have not learned enough of the content taught in English courses, or because they fail to remember and apply what they were previously exposed to.

Traditional English instruction has deep academic roots. Therefore it is not surprising that, among the many varieties of training programs used in business and government, those intended to teach better writing are the most blurred by academe's myopia concerning the differences between cognition and behavior. Nobody would expect a person to play the piano after attending lectures on music, or to scuba dive safely and comfortably after reading the manual. Yet many accept the academic premise that writing, like history, physics, or economics, can be taught as a body of knowledge.

What the visiting trainer *knows,* whether from formal education or on-the-job experience, is not really that relevant. What he or she can help other people *do* at work following training is what matters. But lecturing on one's own knowledge is such an ingrained teaching behavior that writing continues to be taught as a subject to be learned rather than a set of behaviors to be mastered. The results of such instruction are quite predictable—the perpetuation, unchanged, of whatever writing habits the person brought into the training room, combined with a refreshed awareness that those habits produce "incorrect" and "unsatisfactory" work.

Besides English teachers, management can also turn to two other false allies, "Talkers" and "Coaches," when looking for someone to train people how to write better. Talkers lecture. Coaches correct. One delivers up "course content"; the other conducts "individual evaluations."

Let's look at Talkers first.

People Can't Be Talked into Writing Better

"Each Talker," Consultant said, "claims to offer *better* talk than his competitors. But first things first. If someone can demonstrate that people's writing skills improved because they sat and listened to *any* talk, then it will be appropriate to address questions of *which* talk is superior."

Talkers generally deliver lectures that sound like dressed up rehashes from the font of all knowledge about writing, the syllabus for Freshman Composition. Yet Talkers find ready new markets among organizations troubled about their writing. To begin with, what Talkers promise to deliver is exactly what senior management is likely to perceive as missing—words. The first assumption is that people are not writing well because nobody sufficiently knowledgeable has yet *told them* how to write well. So managers can readily picture, in a lecturing expert, a quick and simple solution to a performance problem.

Talkers are also easy for management to buy. To begin with, some promise to talk fast; they offer courses that don't take people away from their desks for long. Talkers also tend to be cheap. Some are moonlighting professors whose business overhead is subsidized by the tax payer. Others, requiring only that people be quiet and pay attention, are pleased to perform for large audiences; so their fees can be distributed over many enrollees. The least expensive Talkers come prerecorded on tape or film. They just need to be plugged into a machine and turned on.

Talkers are also easy to buy because they do not threaten to interfere with the real reasons people are writing ineffectively. Given their certainty that bad writing is nothing more than a symptom of a knowledge deficiency, and that it will be solved if the organization pays them to talk in the presence of the writers, they shield management from participation in and responsibility for the organizational evolution that must take place before the Paper Wars can be won.

Coaching Doesn't Work Either

Coaches are brought in by organizations concerned with finding out "what we've been doing wrong." The Coach's basic premise—that people will start writing well if someone shows them how they have been writing badly—makes them especially attractive to those managers who most want safety from the School Bogeys. So Coaches are often hired in preference even to Talkers offering quick and easy solutions.

They are compelling choices because they promise to deliver, in addition to talk, the other traditional mainstay of the English teacher, lots of correction.

Coaches may introduce some new bells and whistles, but their longer-term effect, if any, is to leave an organization worse than they found it, with the most cumbersome and expensive writing practices even more deeply and permanently entrenched.

Picture the Coach at work. She (or he) sits beside a person she has been hired to help, blue pencil in hand, the person's report in front of her. *What the learner has written, her blue pencil will rewrite.* The pencil touches the page and a clumsy, indirect sentence is suddenly transformed into a crisp dependent clause. After being pronounced a common mistake, a vague pronoun disappears, replaced by a clever rewording the writer would never think of himself, and linked by a conjunction he would be unlikely to use. While praise is voiced in passing—"This paragraph reads nicely." "I really like what you did with the introduction." "This is a lot better than your last report"—the blue pencil stays busy, adding and deleting punctuation marks, neatly excising "unnecessary words," and rigorously correcting spelling.

"You make it look so easy," the learner says.

"Oh, it's not difficult, once you get the hang of it," the Coach answers, modestly.

The Coach's competencies have been expertly exhibited. But not transferred.

While both parties would claim that learning has occurred, neither is likely to be aware of what knowledge the blue pencil actually taught, or rather confirmed, as it scurried busily across the page. If the coachee did not know before, he certainly knows now: Writing exposes him to a high danger of visible mistakes, many of which he makes, and the only safety lies in owning the kind of knowledge the Coach owns.

The writer understands he will *never* know what the Coach knows, of course. But he can do his best to imitate her most clearly remembered behaviors. He can cross out. He can shorten. He can rearrange.

He will never innovate, though. He will never tackle the big problems, like redesigning a report format to make it more user friendly or adapting his style to the needs of a more basic reader. The Coach did not empower him to take charge of his own writing. She gave him permission only to fuss and take care.

Because her instruction confirmed weaknesses he already suspected; because she treated him with patience and gentleness in spite of his manifest guilt; because—in taking upon herself and her trusty blue pencil responsibility for seeking out and correcting his errors—she excused him from involvement in his own learning; because, in making improvement so impossibly difficult and complicated, she absolved him from change; he will sing her praises when asked to evaluate her work.

Instructors who get such feedback on their methods are unlikely to question their results. Neither are those who hire them. So Coaches often become entrenched institutions in organizations they work for, even while the written communications practices they were hired to correct continue to clog and frustrate. As their students testify, "Now at least we know what we're doing wrong."

Behind the polished critiquing techniques of the Coach hides the second big secret of traditional writing instruction: English teachers not only have little to say that is useful *before* people start writing, they do their best work—error spotting—only *after people have written unsuccessfully.*

As a result, Coaches don't in fact teach people how to write successful documents. They teach them how to patch up failed documents.

Why People's Writing Does Improve, Some

"Wait a minute," someone once objected. "We brought in an outside consulting firm. They lectured and coached our people, and we started seeing some improvements."

"Here we are talking errors of magnitude, not of fact," Consultant responded. "Almost any course of instruction, if it includes hands-on learning, will produce *some* improvements in *some* people's performance, if only because of the if-anybody's-watching-I'll-try-harder principle (in Psych 101 it's called the Hawthorne effect).

"The question to ask, following a writing workshop, is not, *Can we see some improvements?* The question to ask is, *Are people now writing helpful, focused documents that contribute to achieving our organization's goals?* In most cases, unfortunately, the answer is no.

"Again we're back to the problem of management expectations," Consultant said. "That BoG has for so long proven invulnerable to most training programs is not surprising. Those programs are not designed to attack the problem of bad writing; they are intended solely to comfort management. Because they reteach what has always been taught— because they refresh people's memory of the many mistakes that can be made and reaffirm the need to try, at least, to avoid them—most courses promise *safe* writing, not *good* writing. Like hanging mistletoe over the door, bringing in a writing course is simply a ceremony managers perform to keep the spooks out.

"And why should management have any higher expectations?" Consultant added. "No one (until now, at least) has ever told them that their organization can, in fact, write successfully—that their employees can become fully competent to turn out functional documents requiring no apology whatsoever. The so-called authorities have *never* given business and government permission to write successfully; they have acknowledged only that people, if they obey the Shoulds and avoid the Mights, can continue writing unsuccessfully, but within safe limits. That is why, even after the same program has been run repeatedly, or after a succession of fully credentialed programs has passed through, BoG still reigns. No one, including those who teach the courses, expects major improvements, only *some* improvements.

"Most training, because it focuses on correcting 'what's wrong with our writing,' nourishes the Bogeys—Corporate, Profession, and School—and further isolates the damaged Writer Within. Therefore it serves but to perpetuate BoG and block CleaR. Only training that frees the Writer and integrates it with the adult Reader Within can help win the Paper Wars."

Writers Teaching Writing

Talkers and Coaches are not the only people management enlists from outside as allies in the Paper Wars. Writers, especially, turn up unexpectedly, and sometimes with the highest sponsorship. The chairman, finally desperate, asks for help from his speech writer or public relations firm. The president, impressed by the clarity and directness of the latest best seller on business management, hires its author to reveal his writing secrets to the staff. Someone's neighbor's daughter, who after all graduated with honors in English and has almost published some short stories, needs work. Professionals such as accountants and engineers often turn to authorities in their own fields, the people whose books and articles demonstrate they write a form of BoG that satisfies that profession's special Bogeys. In one exotic case, an actor who once played a journalist on television was hired to narrate the contents of a training film on how to write.

In the end, it may matter less who is hired than why. If the real intention is to reaffirm "the way we do things around here," BoG needs the protection of neither amateurs nor professionals. It is not only self-perpetuating but extremely durable. It can look after itself.

If, on the other hand, the objective is to replace BoG with CleaR, allies must be chosen carefully, and for the same reason. BoG is charmed against ordinary weapons and will repulse the attacks of all but the most seasoned, skillful, and original troops. CleaR can be taught. But it must be taught carefully and well.

Before I go on, in the next chapter, to talk about solutions that *will* work, I'll pass on a story Consultant told me about a vice president who, having an unusual motive for perpetuating BoG, succeeded in blocking a potential Paper Wars victory.

The Day Consultant Got a Bad Reputation

Sometimes executives can choose the right ally, then give that ally the wrong mission. What they actually want to accomplish can be, sometimes, surprising.

It was a poignant moment.

One of the executives attending the consulting session— a blunt, up-through-the-ranks line manager who had earlier come into the room scowling, jaw set—turned to the Vice President of Manufacturing.

"Is this the kind of writing you want?" he asked, waving his copy of the sheet they were all holding.

"That's exactly the kind of writing I want," the VP answered.

"Why didn't you just say so?"

A sigh went through the room. The tension eased. At the front of the room Consultant, showing a poker face, smiled inwardly. Young Consultant, monitoring the session from behind the backs of the half-dozen managers, grinned broadly.

A long road had led to that moment.

Weeks before, Young Consultant had been invited to fly in (at her firm's expense) to talk with the training coordinator. The problem: "Our line managers are complaining that the Vice President thinks everyone should be Shakespeares. With the VP's enthusiastic concurrence, they've instructed me to find someone to train their people to write reports that will make him happy."

When Young Consultant called her distant boss to describe the project, both she and Consultant were elated. The client was a large and prospering heavy equipment manufacturer, and all the signs indicated they were getting an opportunity to work under the direct sponsorship of a lit vice president. The job would be a piece of cake. Meet with the VP, get his concurrence on the objectives to be achieved by the training, then suggest he instruct the training coordinator to schedule the needed workshops. The coordinator had said that about 300 people would have to be trained, so the project would be lucrative.

But three impediments turned up immediately.

First, senior vice presidents of Fortune 500 corporations do not meet with junior consultants, even for projects near to their hearts. They meet only with senior consultants, preferably from far away, and very carefully.

Second, the line managers were not going to invest time and money sending people to a training program until assured that the program would achieve their sole objective, getting the VP off their necks.

Third, the line managers were absolutely not going to become involved themselves, even though they were the ones who, caught in the middle, had been editing their subordinates' reports in a doomed attempt to meet the VP's standards. As far as they were concerned, the VP should just tell someone what he wanted. That someone should tell their people what the VP wanted. And they themselves should be left alone to get their real work done.

As often is the case when writing is involved, ingenuity was required. The training coordinator arranged for Senior Consultant to fly in from 1,500 miles away (at his firm's expense) so they could "discuss the problem." The meeting was arranged for a day the VP was scheduled to be in town, and it was tacitly agreed that, "if available," he would meet Consultant at lunch. Young Consultant was allowed to tag along.

Coming in on an early flight, Consultant and Young Consultant spent the morning in lackadaisical conversation with the training coordinator while they waited for official confirmation the VP was, in fact, available for lunch. They ended up rushing to the executive dining room with ten minutes' notice.

Working fast between courses, Consultant:

a. Confirmed objectives with the VP.
b. Convinced him that nothing substantive could be achieved as long as the line managers thought *he* was the problem. Their attention needed to be turned from his criticisms to the real problem, the ways their people were writing.
c. Therefore, Consultant proposed, the next step should be a problem-analysis and goal-setting session attended by the VP, the line managers, the training coordinator, and Consultant, who served as leader (this time for a fee and expenses).

Young Consultant was again to be allowed to tag along, as she would later be conducting the training to be planned at the session.

Several weeks later both Consultants arrived on the last flight before a blizzard closed the airport. They brought with them a carefully planned strategy for getting everyone lined up behind the VP on the issue of BoG versus CleaR, a strategy that started unraveling as soon as they entered the meeting room the next morning.

As they were being introduced to the participants (including a quiet younger man identified only as Ted), someone announced that the VP would not arrive until after lunch.

The morning dragged. Consultant stretched, until noon, projects originally scheduled to wrap up before 11:00. Bringing the line managers to a moment of recognition on the gut issues was pointless unless the VP was there to endorse, in person, the new objectives the group would subsequently set. Nevertheless, by lunch the line managers had loosened up considerably. Empowered by their successes during a series of diagnostic projects, they had learned that they themselves could recognize the differences between good and bad writing, and that they themselves were frustrated by the muddy reports their subordinates had been submitting. Discovering that they, too, had something to gain from good writing, they were ready to change sides in the Paper Wars.

But after lunch, with the VP there, the group refroze. Their successes of the morning forgotten, the line managers again faced their real problem, the authority figure whose cryptic, blue-penciled comments made them relive the emotions they felt as schoolboys when corrected by the English teacher.

Not knowing what else to do, Consultant reviewed for the VP the work the group had done that morning and the conclusions they had reached. Reassured by the VP's nods of approval, the line managers began to regain their confidence. Keeping his fingers crossed, Consultant passed out copies of what was intended as the *tour de force* of the session: the Choices page. The page illustrated, in one column, the BoG style people in the company had been writing.

In a matching column it illustrated the same ideas expressed in CleaR, the direct language the VP said he wanted.

Consultant had barely started explaining the Choices page when the big moment came.

"Is this the kind of writing you want?"

"It's exactly the kind of writing I want."

"Well why didn't you just say so? I don't see any problem in getting our people to write like this."

*   *   *   *   *

Several months later, by chance, at an airport a thousand miles away, Consultant met one of the line managers from the session.

"We were disappointed," Consultant said. "We thought we'd be invited back to do some training for you."

"Well, I have to be frank with you. Several people were unhappy with your presentation."

"Oh? What was the problem?"

"They felt the morning session really dragged, especially since, if you had just given us that sheet about BoG and CleaR first thing, we could have sorted everything out in fifteen minutes."

"Well . . . umm . . . has anything been done as a result of our meeting?"

"Oh, sure, we've done something. We went ahead with a training program."

"A training program?"

"Yes. Do you remember Ted, the quiet young fellow sitting near the window? He's a technical writer in our Product Development group. The VP said that with 300 people to train, there was no way we could afford your program. Besides, it lasts too long. We couldn't spare our people for the two days your report writing course takes. But Ted got enough from the materials you handed out in your session to put together a half-day course of our own. Almost everyone has taken it by now."

(Pause.)

"So, what have the results been? Is the Vice President happy?"

"No, and that's probably the main reason you ended up with a bad reputation with us. He's being his old, miserable self. The other line managers and I still spend hours polishing up our people's reports before we send them to him, and he still sends them back all marked up. He figures that hiring you was a waste of time and money."

*   *   *   *   *

When Consultant told this story one Friday afternoon as he, another colleague, and I sipped our second Scotch on the rocks, our friend said, "The Vice President was a closet English teacher."

"What?" Consultant asked.

"He got his jollies marking up people's papers. The real solution to the problem, at least to the problem as the line managers perceived it, might have been to get him a job teaching an evening course in composition at the local community college. Then maybe he'd get it out of his system."

"But if he liked grading papers and wanted to keep doing it, why did he take a chance by bringing us in?"

"The managers called his bluff. They challenged him to put up or shut up."

"Now I see it," Consultant said. "They forced him to make public the kind of writing he wanted. He couldn't explain it, so he had to call us in to speak for him."

"Right. But he wasn't about to let you stay long enough to do any good. He was having too much fun the way things were."

CHAPTER 10

TEACHING PEOPLE
TO WRITE WELL

---

*Organizations must assure that their
employees become self-directing,
fully competent writers.*

"I've got a problem."

"What's that?" Consultant asked.

"Following your instructions, I've told executives what's
wrong with all the ways they've tried to fix bad writing. I
don't seem to have left them with much hope. According to
you, they can't edit. They can't legislate. They can't even
train."

"Of course managers can edit, legislate, and train. But
they have to integrate their own Inner Writers and Readers
first. The problem isn't what they've been doing, but how
and why. As long as their Writers believe in the Bogeys and
won't listen to their Readers, *anything* they do will perpetuate the old destructive lessons. But once they've achieved
their own integration, then they will start sponsoring good
writing, start selecting the right kind of help, and start winning the Paper Wars."

Consultant went on to explain the constructive guidance
people need if they are to become writers of CleaR. He said I
should talk about three things: What the objective of the improvement program must be; what people need to learn; and
how they can best learn it.

Achieving Competence, Not Hedging Failure, Must Be the Objective

"Any job people are capable of doing, they are capable of mastering," Consultant said. "Most white-collar adults can learn to write clear and purposeful business documents, in a short time and with a reasonable effort. Any consultant or teacher who doesn't know—and believe—that should not be allowed to teach the subject. A course of instruction undertaken to help achieve the predominance of CleaR in the organization must, as its first objective, assure that the employees of that organization become *self-directing, fully competent writers.*

"You've already shown, in the war stories you've told, the consequences of withholding permission for people to be competent writers. In perpetuating their dependence on, and vulnerability to, vaguely defined notions of correctness and appropriateness, organizations assure that people imitate whatever form of writing seems to offer the most safety. Thus not only do the various Bogeys go unchallenged, but the writing of the least venturesome and most hesitant becomes the model to which others aspire."

"Self-directing, fully competent writers?" I wondered. "And how many decades are you going to allow for that?"

"Decades? I'm talking about *days,* not decades. I know trainers who can achieve that objective consistently in three days; they can even do a pretty good job in two if they have to."

"Don't you think," I ventured, "that you and I should be concerned about our credibility? How do you expect me to convince my readers that they or anyone else can become a good and independent writer in two or three days?"

"I don't think we have to convince them of anything," he answered. "People I work with have been achieving that goal for almost two decades, as some 50,000 former workshop participants can attest. You don't have to explain that the job *can* be done, just *how* it's done."

"Hmm . . . So, tell me what to say."

Building Upon, Rather than Putting In

According to Consultant, the first mistake most writing instructors make is to think they *know* something other people need to know. "As you explained earlier," he said, "every working adult has within a warehouse that is bulging with the Inner Reader's lifetime accumulation of knowledge about writing. The purpose of training should be to help the Writer within each person open that warehouse and put those resources to use—not to put the workshop leader's knowledge on parade."

Therefore, he went on, training others to become competent, independent writers is a matter of putting them in touch with *what they already know,* and then of *giving them permission to use it.*

People who write good business documents do so, first, because they are competent in their fields. They know what matters and what doesn't. They have sufficient professional knowledge and experience to decide what needs to be said in a report to assure it does the job intended—*if* they have freed their Writer from its old preoccupation with what one is "supposed to say."

Secondly, good business writers make constructive choices about the ways they perform some half-dozen or so primary competencies required by organizational writing. These choices, which result in documents being written in CleaR, are straightforward practices that can be described objectively and discussed in grown-up, nonjudgmental ways (as previous chapters have demonstrated).

"I'm not talking about rules," Consultant said. "A person can never know enough rules to write either well or safely. I am talking about decisions adults can make about the ways they put words down on paper." He went on to explain that people should be guided in their choices by the effects they want their documents to have (not judgments they think "experts" have made about what is "correct" or "acceptable").

If made aware of their alternatives, grown-ups can elect, for example, to build documents from an early and explicit purpose declaration, and they can elect to build paragraphs and sections from overview or theme statements. (Or, conversely, they can choose to continue the BoG practice of constructing elaborate cases before letting their readers in on what they are getting at. But once they've felt the freedom of the more assertive practices, few elect to continue making the old choices.)

As to style, they can elect to write CleaR sentences that communicate ideas in concrete images readers can comprehend directly (rather than continuing to write concept statements, abstractions that readers can penetrate only by translating them into what they likely mean). Instead of habitually hedging, they can elect to state those things they know to be true and explicitly qualify those they are unsure of. They can choose to step forward, in their writing, and say what they think (rather than choosing to quibble and qualify, hoping the reader will not be offended when he finally figures out what they are hinting at).

"So good training," Consultant insists, "helps people's Inner Reader put them in touch with their alternatives when they write. And it frees their Inner Writer to make the clearest, most helpful choices."

Managing How People Learn

"So how is this feat pulled off?" I asked. "Explain how trainers can help people understand their choices and give them permission to make the right ones."

"First, we have to look at the whole question of training-room time and the uses to which it is put," he began. The explanation that followed turned out to be more convincing than I expected.

It seems that a teacher's primary task is to structure *other people's activities* in ways that result in learning. Massive amounts of learning can be accomplished in two or three days by teachers who have taken to heart an absolute law: *Only learner behavior results in learning.* The teacher may speak, but to no avail unless the learner listens. The teacher may show, but to understand and remember the learner must see. We learn from what *we do,* not from what *someone else does.*

People learn by performing five specific behaviors, each behavior having a predictable efficiency:

1. Of what they *read,* people remember approximately 5 percent.
2. Of what they *hear,* they remember approximately 10 percent.
3. Of what they *see,* they remember approximately 30 percent.
4. Of what they *say,* they remember approximately 35 percent.
5. Of what they *do,* they remember approximately 50 percent.

The highest level of learning efficiency comes when saying and doing are combined—people's retention rate approaches 75 percent when they *do* a task, then *talk* to someone about how they did it.

According to Consultant, this learning model, and the accompanying percentages, appeared many years ago in the magazine, *Training HRD.* "I loaned out my copy and it was never returned," he said. "I do not know what data exists to support the percentages, but to me they have the feel of deep truth. Nothing I have experienced as either a learner or a teacher would lead me to question their essential (if not statistical) validity."

This list is fun to play with. We can use it, for example, to explain the old saying, "If you ever want to really learn a subject, teach it." As the list shows, traditionally teachers have performed the high-efficiency learning behaviors—*doing* and *saying*—while their students have sat *listening* and *watching*.

The list also accounts for the modern-day growth of visual-based learning such as slides, films, and videos. The instructional function may still be seen as "content dumping," but visually dumped content is absorbed three times more efficiently than orally dumped content.

As well, the chart explains why those who attend conferences (educational and training conferences, at least) no longer listen to so many speakers. Instead, they now spend much of their time participating in structured group discussions managed by the featured celebrities. The thinking of the session leaders is irrefutable: There's no point in their talking at a 10 percent teaching efficiency when the participants themselves can talk at a 35 percent learning efficiency. (Some complaints have been heard, of course. "She's a well-known expert in my field, and I came to the conference to hear her speak. If I wanted to listen to myself talk, I could have stayed home with my cat.")

The list of learning behaviors also suggests some conclusions about our own communications behaviors. If the matter is important—if we need to assure that others receive and take ownership of certain information—we can't risk just telling them. And we certainly can't risk posting a notice on the bulletin board or circulating a memo. An assured failure rate of 90 to 95 percent is a long shot at anybody's track. The same applies to teaching. Given the learning efficiency percentages, the fact that something was "covered" in a lecture is not even sufficient grounds for claiming people *may* know it. And anything set aside for the evening reading to teach should be considered a write-off.

Consultant disagrees, incidentally, with academics who claim that, by passing final examinations in university courses, people demonstrate they learn substantial amounts from lectures and assigned readings. He says that as examination time approaches, most conscientious students rework their lecture notes; they go through the reading again and make additional notes; perhaps they even get together among themselves and discuss the course content. In other words, they start *doing,* and sometimes even *doing and saying.* These are learning behaviors which give them some ownership, however temporary, of the course content delivered by the instructor.

"Therefore," Consultant once said, "you can safely bet your royalties against an academic's increments that, in a learning experiment offering no motive to cram, testing won't recover any meaningful amount of his lectures from a significant number of his students."

If Consultant will not grant writing teachers permission to talk, what will he let them do? To begin with, he says they *can* talk. Just not nearly as much, and for entirely different reasons. He says the first step in becoming an effective teacher of writing is to accept two realities:

1. There's no point in talking in the classroom, because people will remember only an unpredictable 10 percent of what you say; and
2. 80 percent of the traditional writing course content is only time-filler anyway.

Consultant also pointed out a third reality: "When you are talking, people are not learning—they are *preparing to learn.* Like students sitting in a lecture hall, they are only setting the parameters of their future learning task—the one they intend to postpone until examination time comes."

This habit of *deferred* learning, he explained, is why everyone has been able to pretend, for so many years, that "absorption" takes place at a time *after* the formal instruction; that people carry away the instructor's words and *later,* by some unexplained process, make them their own. But as we have seen, forgetting, discounting, and failure are the effects of time on learning, not consolidation and ownership.

Consultant's solution, therefore, is quite simple. "Stop performing all those *teacher behaviors* that we know produce a low level of learning. Then, having freed up our allotted time for other uses, we can schedule for the training room *the learner behaviors—doing and saying—that we know result in the permanent acquisition of new skills.*"

In short, any minute the workshop leader refrains from talking, the course participants can spend doing—writing, in other words. And if they are given a chance to critique their work for the instructor (rather than have the instructor critique it for them), they multiply the learning effects of *doing* by *saying* as well. They will therefore take ownership of the new skills immediately (not at some hypothetical time in the future).

"Wait a minute," I interrupted. "What you've said about people learning from their own actions—rather than from a teacher's actions—makes a lot of sense. But if writing is the behavior that teaches good writing . . . and if people already spend 20 percent or more of their working time turning out memos, letters, reports, and what not, why don't they just become better writers automatically?"

"Writing isn't the activity that teaches better writing," he answered. "*Better* writing is."

"What?"

"Better writing is the only activity that teaches better writing."

"You'd better take over," I said, motioning him to my seat at the keyboard.

Consultant Explains, in His Own Words, How to Teach People to Write CleaR

Training that helps people integrate their Inner Reader with their Inner Writer is a powerful weapon in the hands of managers who are determined to win the Paper Wars. But to achieve that objective, training must meet three minimum specifications, and must meet them rigorously.

1. *People must spend most of their course time writing.* By most, I mean they should spend 80 percent or more of their workshop time, pens in hand, writing. And by writing, I mean composing original, full-length documents, not filling in the blanks while *re*writing exercises supplied by the instructor (not even exercises supposedly "customized" from client-supplied documents).

2. *People must write successfully.* The purpose of the writing assignments must *not* be to produce flawed documents for the instructor to correct. The assignments must be designed to assure that most of the documents written by most of the trainees are fully adequate for their intended business purposes. And success must be achieved during the course, not at some hypothetical time afterwards.

3. *People must know they have written successfully, and must be able to explain why.* There is no point in teaching people to write to the satisfaction of a workshop leader, then have that leader go away. The training must give people thorough, explicit, and realistic criteria for judging their own writing; further, it must assure they are able to apply the criteria, confidently and consistently, to the writing they will be doing in the weeks and months following the course.

The problem of assuring that people write *successfully,* and that they know *why* and *how* they did it, is not really difficult to solve. The workshop leader, by giving carefully crafted directions, can initiate assignments that will assure people write good documents (not faulted documents that need teacher correction). The directions must be clear. They must be brief. They must have no purpose other than to guide the work of the learners during the project immediately to follow. (That is, direction giving—now that the instructor is finally allowed to talk—should not be taken as an opportunity for him to display either his marvelous sense of humor or his ability to elaborate simple ideas into complicated systems.) Most important, the directions must be given in words the participants understand—and understand so well they can use themselves.

Now we're back to content. Not the 80 percent that's writing course filler, but the 20 percent that can help people change if it is rethought and properly used. Notice I said "help people change." We must remember that the transfer of cognitive information about writing should *never* be the objective of the course—*stimulating the confident performance of new and more effective writing behaviors, both during the training and afterwards, must always be the objective of the course.*

In order to deliberately change their behaviors, people must first acquire understanding of both their present behaviors and their new alternatives. They can achieve this understanding by learning new perceptions, plus a vocabulary for naming those perceptions. But people can build learning upon new perceptions and a working vocabulary only if the perceptions and words become their own. They have to be given permission to take command of, and use confidently, both their new ways of perceiving and their exciting new ability to talk about what they see and do.

So the instructor has to be prepared not only to teach the competencies, but to surrender ownership of them as well. Perhaps English teachers more than most have seemed jealous of their mysteries. Motivated by a sincere, though misplaced, loyalty to their subject matter, they habitually elaborate simple concepts into indigestible lumps of rules and exceptions. They insist upon thorough and often hairsplitting correction, both on paper and during discussions.

No wonder, then, people so readily assume that only an advanced degree in English qualifies a person to deal competently with writing. The person who leaves a workshop having been taught that, even after all these years, he still cannot (and should be able to) spot a dangling modifier, also leaves the workshop having confirmed any sense of ignorance and inadequacy he may have started with. He spent the course with his nose pressed to the window. Whatever he saw there still belongs to the course leader. "No, I'm still not writing any better. But I sure would be if I could do all the things she told us to do."

Thus the function of content must be to help people learn, not to help the instructor teach. Once people have themselves learned words for describing their alternatives as writers, they can understand the workshop leader's instructions. They can talk with the leader during the projects. And following the projects, they can explain to the leader and other course participants what they have done and why. That is how people take ownership and become independent, fully competent writers.

Here is the training room picture we now have: The workshop leader delivers brief (two to five minute) carefully crafted instructions. Directed by those instructions, the course participants spend a much longer time (perhaps twenty minutes to two or more hours) completing a project. During that time the leader doesn't have much to do. Now she, rather than the students, is watcher and listener. If someone asks her a question; if someone obviously is struggling but seems too shy to say so; she should then intervene. But she should *never* try to solve the learner's problem. Instead, she should ask them to talk about their own alternatives for solving it.

And when each project is finished, the leader's principal role is to listen and acknowledge while the course participants explain what they did during the assignment and why it was successful. Given instructor patience and self-restraint, the problem of negative feedback solves itself under this scenario. When learners make unwise choices, *they* will usually recognize what they should have done instead. And—if the instructor can resist the urge to leap in with correction—they will explain how they will do it differently next time.

Teaching writing to experienced, working adults is not a matter of instilling as many new ideas as the instructor can verbalize in the time allowed. It is a matter of releasing the vast language resources that people have already acquired during their life times. Grown-ups can learn, in just a few days, to become competent, self-directing business or technical writers. But they need an instructional program that is sufficiently disciplined to eliminate the two most ego-satisfying roles the English teacher plays: lecturing and correcting.

The program must be taught consistently, as well. One of the more common complaints I hear is, "The firm (or college) that conducts our writing courses keeps sending us different instructors. Every instructor teaches a different course." A workshop must be designed to teach a specific set of competencies, and every presentation should teach them all, thoroughly and exclusively, regardless of who is instructing. The notion that each writing teacher has some special knowledge to impart is nothing but an academic self-indulgence.

So, *if* the workshop leader opts for teaching instead of talking, *if* those attending write successfully, and can explain why, and *if* the course addresses the fundamental issues of written communications (rather than the cosmetic issues of "correctness"), a training program in writing can help win the Wars by installing the skills an organization needs in order to supplant BoG with CleaR. However, no program is good enough, no consultant skilled enough, to eliminate BoG unless management wants it eliminated.

It's Not Over When It's Over

"Then what happens?" I asked, as I returned to my keyboard.

"What do you mean?"

"After the training program? What happens then?"

"Oh," Consultant said. "Then managers have to look for, and be prepared to support, the immediate results that will follow."

"Immediate results! There you go again."

"I'm not exaggerating," he said. *"Training produces either immediate results, or none.* People either return to work ready to try out, on the job, new skills, or they resume their old ways of doing things and start forgetting everything they did in the course."

"So you're proposing they are going to come back from training as perfectly competent writers."

Consultant looked exasperated. "I'm proposing no such thing. I'm proposing that—if the training program actually did its job, and if management has clearly signaled it wants change—people will immediately start *experimenting* with the new ways of writing. Certainly the results aren't going to be perfect. Just the opposite, in fact. Anyone who risks trying new writing techniques is going to make some mistakes. False starts and misapplications are predictable at that stage of learning.

"So managers have to be careful," he warned. "Their first impression may be that the workshop only replaced the old errors with new ones. And their first impulse may be to start stomping on people. So now is when executives have to do their most careful—and perhaps most unfamiliar—work."

"Such as?"

"They have to ask friendly questions about writing, like 'I'm not sure I understand why you started the memo this way. Is this something you learned in the workshop?' And they have to risk opening up. 'I'm not comfortable about the change, but I'm interested in hearing what you're trying to do.'

"Most of all, they have to silence their own threatened Bogeys; otherwise they'll conjure the employees' Bogeys. The boss who says, 'This isn't the way we do it,' or 'You can't say that—it's *too* clear,' should have the cost of the training program deducted from his pay check. He's just wiped out its effects."

Taking the Mickey out of BoG

Consultant says the Paper Wars are surprisingly easy to win. For all its seeming potency, BoG has only one source of power—old fears. The day executives recognize that *BoG is not essential to their safety* its grip on the organization immediately loosens. And when they acknowledge *how bad BoG is making them look,* it quickly starts to become a faded memory, something to pull from the old files and chuckle over—or wince at—now and then.

CHAPTER 11

PAYING THE PRICE

*So much for so little. . . . But you have to
be prepared to take some lumps. And
you've got to get into the game yourself.*

You've Got to Make It Happen

If you hold a responsible position in a corporation or agency,
Consultant and I are offering a deal you can't refuse. If you
do what is needed to eliminate BoG from the writing of your
organization, you won't have to *read* BoG anymore.

And if knowing, every day when you come to work, that
you'll be able to read and understand the stack of paper
waiting on your desk isn't reward enough, there are other
benefits as well. If you start writing CleaR you'll scare your
competitors. You'll impress your customers or clients. And
you'll bring smiles to the faces of your stockholders (or your
politicians). You'll even make your employees happier.

So much for so little. In order to win the Paper Wars,
you only have to install people's Inner Readers, rather
than their Bogeys, in charge of your organization's written
communications. But to do that, you have to be prepared
to take some lumps. And you've got to get into the game
yourself. The BoG problem belongs to all of us, not someone else. Each of us is a potential blocker of change, even
if inadvertently.

Why Change Feels Like an Injury

It's a good thing the human organism is so resistant to
change. If we didn't have our internal Change Stoppers, we

would never remember. We would not even have personalities. Mentally and emotionally we would simply exist in a perpetual state of amoebic flux, reorganizing ourselves in response to each new stimulus. That is why we take change so seriously. It threatens our integrity of being, everything we know and are.

When threatened with externally imposed change, we are never without reasons, or rationalizations, at least, for resisting. As to voluntary change, we prefer to take our own sweet time and to preserve as much of our original investment as possible. That's why people prefer to *taper off* smoking, or *try* to quit. More is at stake than their nicotine addiction.

Our built-in resistance to change is what makes *improvement* so surprisingly difficult for us, even when it's clearly to our benefit. No changes to the ways we work, even positive ones, are free. Established behaviors will not leave without a fight, and new ones must always prove themselves both safe and worth the cost before being adopted.

So as soon as CleaR starts supplanting BoG, everyone—even those most avidly sponsoring the improvement—must deal with some very real feelings of discomfort. Let's look at a couple of the primary changes that must occur, and what they will feel like.

One BoG practice is to delay telling readers *why* we've written until we have told them practically everything else. The reward for persisting in that behavior is the comfort we feel that we'll get a fair hearing, that the reader will *have* to listen to our whole case before she gets an opportunity to pass judgment on what we are up to. The truth, of course, is that we have no control over what the reader does with our letter. If she's experienced, she may skip right to the end to find out what we want. If she's inexperienced, she may set the letter aside. "No, I couldn't figure out what that letter was going on about, so I chucked it." A third scenario: She'll dig her way through, mentally squirreling away everything we say until she's finally figured out what we're leading up to, all the time muttering about "wind bags who beat around the bush."

So one new change you'll have to adopt (and allow others to adopt) is the consistent practice of including in the introduction to every document an explicit statement of what you want the reader to do or know as a result of reading it. *Every* document, *especially* the most scary ones.

The payoff will be immediate. Your letters, memos, and reports will not only be much shorter, they will start producing the results you want, much more consistently and with fewer follow-up clarifications. But your Change Stoppers will start punishing you immediately too. "You're not supposed to do that. You can't just come right out and tell them what you want. They might say no before they've even read your letter."

Another necessary change will be a shift to writing in basic English. No more hiding behind a "professional," or a "dignified," or a "businesslike" style. Your readers will love you for it; they'll decide that maybe you're not so stuffy after all. But your Change Stoppers will make you feel vulnerable. "If you make it sound that simple, they'll think you're an idiot." "You're an educated man, but if you write like that, no one will be able to tell." "For what you're paid, surely you can make it sound more complicated than that."

Fortunately, change resistance is often nothing more than the human organism's discomforting overreaction to something new. It is, by its very nature, temporary. We replace bad habits with good ones by performing new, more beneficial behaviors. As soon as we've repeated them a few times they become familiar to our Change Stoppers, who then claim the new ways as their own and become as ferocious in their defense as they were before in attacking them.

But you have to reward yourself for your new writing practices. Enjoy and celebrate the benefits of being an individual (and an organization) capable of turning out direct, confident documents that do what they are supposed to do. The moment you hesitate—the moment you wonder, "Yes, but is this the way we're *supposed* to write?"—the old habits will come crawling out of their nooks and crannies and promise to make you feel safe once again.

The Insurance Adjusters Try to Change

Consultant is a scarred Paper Wars veteran. But he had never before been caught in the cross fire between two platoons of Bogeymen who were fighting each other. And not until a couple of years later, looking back on the case, did he spot the secret agents who had lured him into the ambush.

Startled when the firing broke out, his first instinct was escape. But there was no where to run. He had spent the morning of the one-day workshop for some 50 or 60 insurance adjusters doing diagnostic and motivation projects intended to unfreeze them in preparation for change. But now he was suddenly in the midst of a battle. People were arguing with each other, and with him, about some changes he had just proposed they make in their reports. According to the battle plan he had brought into the room, he should by this point have taken them all prisoner without firing a shot. Instead he was crouching in a crater in no man's land with shells from both sides bursting around him. The afternoon looked unpromising.

The afternoon was, in fact, a disaster. The morning projects had been designed to help people come to agreement on the need to tackle certain problems. In the projects planned for the afternoon, they were to work together trying out, and taking ownership of, some solutions to those problems. But the model provided no contingency for the situation Consultant had walked into blindly. In spite of careful probing in advance, and in spite of monitoring the morning's discussions with some care, he discovered only now that the room contained two factions, and that each faction thought the "real problem" was the writing practices of the other. Consultant suddenly realized that one faction, without telling him, had hired him to set the other faction straight, the sort of scenario that makes change agents wake in the night in a cold sweat.

As Consultant later pieced together the details, he recognized the client organization had been going through a commonplace internal crisis. A small and aggressive company (we'll call it Adjusta Inc.) had recently bought out one of its larger competitors. Each firm had its own set of report writing precedents and its own Corporate Bogeys to enforce them. The executives of Adjusta Inc., being the new owners, understandably thought their ways should now constitute everybody's standard practices.

Their heavy-handed method for instituting the changeover, and the unintended consequences, were also familiar. A committee codified Adjusta Inc.'s traditional practices in a policies and procedures manual and declared them *the* way things were now to be done. Resentment, resistance and noncompliance predictably followed.

So management decided to call in outside help, not realizing that getting their way would be far more difficult now that they had tried to impose the manual on people. They approached Consultant who, after examining some examples of reports written by the rebellious employees, conveniently proposed approximately the same changes the manual had decreed. So he was hired.

But why, Consultant puzzled afterward, hadn't he been told? He had simply been asked to run a workshop in conjunction with one of their twice yearly general meetings. Even when he explained what he intended to accomplish in the session and probed for potential resistance, he didn't get a hint, not the slightest intimation, that there was discord, or that steps had already been taken, unsuccessfully, to change the way some people wrote their reports. The nearest he came to learning of the dispute was when, the night before the session, someone handed him a thick binder and casually suggested, "Perhaps you'd like to take a look at our new policy and procedures manual before tomorrow."

Only much later did Consultant realize that he'd been set up by another group of spooks—the Profession Bogeys who haunt the *talk* of insurance adjusters. Adjusters usually gather the facts for their reports, and the insights they need to interpret them, by interviewing distraught people, victims of or witnesses to misfortune or even disaster. Therefore adjusters' speech practices have to reassure, to comfort. Because they must promise succor before they know what they can commit to, they have mastered the political arts of deflecting direct questions and avoiding direct responses. "Trust me," they've learned to make their voices say. "In time all will be made well."

In other words, the Adjusta Inc. executives, being insurance adjusters, were prevented by their speech Bogeys from admitting what their writing Bogeys had been up to. Consultant never had a chance.

Sending Yourself In

No one can be a hero in the invasion unless he gets on the boat. You'll never win the Paper Wars if you start off by benching yourself.

You have to get involved. If you're the boss, you need to set the example. Decide what needs to be changed, then change it in your own writing first. Sponsor CleaR publicly. No one is going to risk writing it until they're sure you're on their side. You absolutely have to give feedback, and it has to be positive. Notice improvement, acknowledge it, and reward it with praise.

You also have to monitor and enforce—forever. BoG has lots of friends out there, and it will be lurking in the shadows watching for openings. Accept no excuses. (There are no valid justifications for BoG.) Accept no delays. (If not now, when?) Accept no exceptions. (If not us, who?) Make the new CleaR standards explicit, and make them stick.

You have to allocate the resources as well. Spend what is needed to get the job done, not what is sufficient to make a convincing gesture. If you decide a training program is needed, and if the best one takes three days, approve three days; don't insist that someone "try to do it" in one or two. And hire the most competent, not the cheapest.

Be especially wary of people peddling Hiding Places and Red Herrings. If someone tells you that you're "absolutely right" about writing, that "our program exactly fits the needs you've just outlined," you're probably being sold, not served. Get someone who will be a little tough with you, who will challenge your assumptions, and who is willing to press you to look at some uncomfortable facts. Being a writing expert is his or her job, not yours.

As the following bit of fiction demonstrates, if you don't launch the campaign against BoG yourself, no one else is likely to.

BoG Fumbled Twice, but Nobody Would Pick Up the Ball and Run

EMPLOYEE:

What do you mean, I write BoG?

DEPARTMENT HEAD:

A friend of mine told me about a book he's just read on the subject. I gather it says that some people write in a way called BoG, and others write in a way called CleaR. From what I understand, CleaR is a lot easier to read. I want you to start writing the reports you send me in CleaR.

EMPLOYEE:

But I write just like you do.

DEPARTMENT HEAD:

You don't understand. I have to write BoG because my reports go to Divisional Manager. It's okay for you to write CleaR. Your reports only come to me.

DIVISIONAL MANAGER:

Wait a minute, Department Head. I want the reports you send me to be written in CleaR, too.

DEPARTMENT HEAD:

Written in CleaR? But we've worked together for years. You're the one who taught me how reports are supposed to be written.

DIVISIONAL MANAGER:

I taught you how reports are supposed to be written for the VP. But when you write them for me, I'd rather have them written in CleaR.

VICE PRESIDENT:

Are you saying, D.M., that the reports *I have to read* should be written in a more difficult style, while the ones *you have to read* should be written in an easier style?

DIVISIONAL MANAGER:

Well . . . I mean . . . after all, you are a vice president.

VICE PRESIDENT:

I think it's time this company took a close look at its written communications. I'm going to bring up this issue at the executive committee meeting.

(Next week, at the executive committee meeting)

PRESIDENT:

I'm glad you raised the matter, Vice President. In fact, it's very timely. The Chairman called me aside last week after the board of director's meeting. Apparently he has just read a book that explains about two different types of business writing. I understand one of them is called BoG, and the other is called CleaR. He says the reports we've been sending to the board have been written in BoG, and he wants us to start writing them in CleaR. Look into it, will you please?

(Later)

VICE PRESIDENT:

Divisional Manager, tell your people. The Chairman says that all reports to the board now have to be written in CleaR.

DIVISIONAL MANAGER:

In CleaR? You mean that kind of writing we were talking about last week?

VICE PRESIDENT:

That's right. And we don't have any choice. What the Chairman wants, the Chairman gets.

(Later)

DIVISIONAL MANAGER:

You really opened a can of worms, didn't you, Department Head?

DEPARTMENT HEAD:

What do you mean?

DIVISIONAL MANAGER:

Now the Chairman is all stirred up about that BoG and CleaR stuff. He's decreed that your reports have to be written in CleaR. See to it.

(Later)

DEPARTMENT HEAD:

Employee, please step into my office.

EMPLOYEE:

Yes sir.

DEPARTMENT HEAD:

Now then. The word has come straight from the top. Directly from the Chairman, in fact. As of this date, every report you submit is to be written in CleaR. Have I made myself understood?

EMPLOYEE:

Yes sir.

DEPARTMENT HEAD:

Good. Now all you have to do is find someone to loan you a copy of that book.

Those in the Middle Can Win the Battles, but Those at the Top Must Win the Wars

"Be sure to tell them," Consultant said, "about the critical and sometimes punishing role played by middle management. Probably the best definition of 'middle management' is 'being caught in the middle.' These are the men and women who must implement change, often in spite of the reluctance of their subordinates, the opposition of their peers, and the indifference of their superiors."

"So you've found that the job of winning the Paper Wars belongs to middle management?"

"Definitely not," Consultant answered. "Middle management can only win or lose the *battles*. Senior management wins or loses the Wars. When senior executives don't integrate their own Writers and Readers, they can defeat all attempts to install CleaR, either through active resistance or benign disinterest."

CHAPTER 12

FIGHTING THE CAMPAIGN

If there is one thing we know about
change, it's that it occurs in
organizations from the top down.

"Has any organization ever won the Paper Wars?" I asked.

"If you mean in the sense of large, diverse organizations, I don't know," Consultant said. "I've certainly known smaller organizations that have, and departments, even divisions, of larger ones. But I've never personally come in contact with a full-sized corporation or agency that even made a serious effort. The will to win the Paper Wars seems lacking at the highest levels. I suspect that management, at heart, simply doesn't believe the Wars *can* be won. They seem to have decided bad writing is a distasteful fact of life, a problem they can neither ignore nor finally solve."

"What would management have to do in order to create an organization that writes purposefully and well? What must happen if the Paper Wars are to be won?"

"First off, of course, management would have to decide they *wanted* to win," he answered. That first step—denying BoG and putting their Bogeys behind them—is the most difficult of all. We can not easily give up deeply held assumptions, even if they are disabling to us.

"Once that first, great hurdle is behind them, then it's just a matter of managing change. They need to understand the campaign and how to wage it."

Consultant then explained that every campaign against BoG proceeds in five steps:

1. Discovering the problem.
2. Setting the objective.
3. Arranging the intervention.
4. Managing the intervention.
5. Making the changes permanent.

"Or to put it another way," he went on, "you can talk about what happens before, during, and after the intervention."

Before the Intervention

Step one of every campaign is the discovery of a problem—or as Consultant calls it, the "somebody has to do something about the way we write" stage. That discovery must be carefully distinguished from the pronouncement, "Somebody *ought* to do something about the way we write." Every day organizations rediscover they *ought* to improve writing. But until someone with sufficient authority says *has to,* the futile struggles against BoG continue.

One such discovery came during the recession of the early '80s, when the president of an international paper products company decided that, because money was hard to come by, the company could no longer afford for him to approve major capital expenditures when he couldn't understand the reports recommending them. So he declared that "something's gotta be done," and a major training program was launched.

Even more overt crises can precipitate the decision. A power company, for instance, suffered through the embarrassment of a public inquiry into massive cost overruns on a major project. Day after day their lawyers had to table badly written engineering reports and explain why work had to be redone, in some cases more than once, because the job-site personnel could not understand the reports.

But usually, Consultant says, the discovery of the problem is less dramatic. Somebody, perhaps having a bad day, finally concludes: "Life at a desk is tough enough. Why should I have to work so hard digging through all this pointless, self-protective verbiage in order to get my hands on the information I need to keep this operation running?"

Once the decision has been made to "do something," the next step is objective setting. Management must decide what results it wants to prevail in place of the problem it has discovered. One large computer manufacturer, for example, discovered its problem when it kept getting the same basic message from its customers. "We're sure we'll find out how marvelous your machines are—if we can ever figure out, from the operator's manual, how to turn them on." So the company researched the people who typically fed data to computers—at that time mostly clerical types with high school diplomas to two years of college. Their surprising discovery: Their user manuals had to be written for people who read, on average, at the sixth grade level. So they set their improvement objective as teaching their computer specialists to write instructions at that level.

As the old saying goes, if you don't know where you're going, any road will do. Yet according to Consultant, step two—the objective-setting stage—is where failure is built into 90 percent of campaigns. Discomfited by the whole subject of writing, management too often skips directly to a supposed solution. "We all know what good writing is. Let's just find a writing course and send our people to it." Or, "Let's set up a committee to put together some guidelines." If running a writing course is decided upon as the objective, it matters little what follows. Any course with the requisite name will serve, and the objective can be declared met when people file out of the training room at the conclusion of the workshop. The same must be said about other hastily set solutions such as "putting together some guidelines." Regardless of what the guidelines say, or of whether anyone ever reads them, the fact they have been published will be taken by some as sufficient evidence the problem of bad writing needs no further attention.

A lot more can be achieved, in the way of changing writing, than managers are likely to think. If they set a *lesser* objective than a significant and permanent improvement in the organization's writing, or if they set a *different* objective than that, they can end up investing in a disappointing intervention. As one executive put it, "I thought the best we could hope for was to bring our poorest writers up to the departmental average. I had no idea that all of us would soon be turning out letters and reports as good as those our best writers produced. Fortunately, we selected a training program that delivered more than we were looking for."

"Nothing," Consultant said, "is more crucial to victory than a clear and worthy objective honestly pursued."

*   *   *   *   *

"Even with a good objective, the sponsors of better writing must still be alert during step three, or selecting the resources for the intervention," Consultant continued. "I call this step, 'Finding the best training program management can be talked into buying.' This stage often mobilizes an organization's BoG defenders. They will argue that the intervention should be confined to the fewest number at the lowest ranks, and that it should be as quick and cheap as possible. They will also attempt to co-opt the intervention in order to assure that promoting safety, rather than accomplishing improvement, becomes its goal. As well, they are likely to prevent—often by carefully rationalized boycott—the creation of knowledgeable and unanimous management support for the intervention's objective."

"In other words," I said, "you're talking about the stage at which so many ineffectual solutions get chosen."

"That's right. This is the Red Herring stage," Consultant replied. "BoG defenders whose approvals are needed to make the project work can, by loading the selection process with false objectives, smoke screen the original goal and divert the intervention from change to preservation.

"This is also the stage at which management often turns the whole matter over to someone else—like the organization's HRD department, for instance. I couldn't count the number of times in the last twenty years I've talked with a training person who had been told to find a writing course, but who had only the sketchiest notion of what management wanted the course to achieve—a fact that may help explain why training departments sometimes seem to be promoting puzzling offerings. Certainly senior managers are not likely to go out shopping for training programs themselves. But they must communicate clear-cut program objectives to the people they delegate to do that leg work.

"And when HRD people return with their recommended selection, they should be expected to explain how the program they've chosen will actually meet the objectives. Trainers may have their own notions about what constitutes a worthy program, and during the selection process goals can emerge that are far different from those set by management. We ran into an instance when the management of a company, after very successfully piloting a writing course, instructed the training department to proceed with a major training program built upon that workshop. When the program went ahead, however, managers discovered their people were attending a different and much less effective course. The original course had been 'deselected' by a trainer who decided it didn't include the requisite proportion of group projects.

"On the other hand," Consultant continued, "management is sometimes guilty of turning the matter over to the HRD department, then sabotaging its work. I remember a carefully planned, precisely targeted program that was dumped at the last minute. Another firm got into the executive suite and started people fussing about the academic credentials of the workshop leader. The company ended up abandoning its program objectives and brought in a Ph.D. whose lectures bored people to tears—and of course had no effect on the writing problems management wanted to solve.

"So managers who launch a campaign against BoG must insist the solution chosen, as a minimum criterion, must help the organization achieve the original objective set for it. Any other goals must be subordinated to that primary one."

During the Intervention

"You'd be amazed," Consultant said, "by how often senior executives who gave serious thought to setting the change objectives, and who carefully monitored the selection of the training program, seem to have forgotten the whole matter when the time comes to make the intervention work."

He went on to explain that a program can be all set to roll, then suddenly everything seems to go wrong. Managers resist approving dates for workshops. Courses get scheduled but people cannot be spared to attend them. When a course does get run, those who most need to be there are the least likely to show up. Someone else gets sent instead. Often trainers have to beat the corporate bushes for warm, available bodies so workshops run at a decent enrollment. People show up for a course asking, "Why am I here?" Then they leave objecting, "My boss will never let me do it." And then there's the dreaded budget cut, or as it's sometimes called, the change in spending priorities. Nothing disappears faster than training programs when management starts looking for ways to reduce expenditures."

Consultant recounted how, with management not paying attention, a major change program almost went awry.

A manufacturer of communications equipment had elected, in the face of fierce competition, to professionalize its sales proposals, so the training department was sent in search of a good workshop on technical proposal writing. The company also decided to teach its people to sell to customer objectives, so the training department was instructed to arrange for training in that area as well. The training person in charge did an excellent job of coordinating the two programs to assure that people learned to use the new selling approach both when meeting with a customer and later when they wrote the proposal.

Almost the entire sales staff had been through both training programs when the regional sales manager decided to conduct a review of the proposals people were sending out. She was dismayed to discover that only *one person* was using the new sales approach and following the new proposal format. An emergency meeting was called, attended by the vice president of marketing, the regional manager, the sales division's middle managers, the training coordinator, and the leaders of both workshops. The surprising discovery to come from the meeting was that middle management—after helping to plan the new selling approach and approving the two training programs that were to put it into effect—had apparently gone back to fighting fires and forgotten about the whole matter. They were chagrined to learn that the training had almost run its course without their support and encouragement.

Their organization, like many others, had not yet formed the habit of thinking of training as a method for creating change. It was just something people were sent to. So people went off to workshops in order to learn new work behaviors, then returned to offices where their bosses carried on just as before. A business-as-usual management attitude quickly undercuts the effects of any change program.

The first decision to come from the meeting of the company's sales executives was that all middle managers would, finally, attend both workshops themselves. Then they would attend a specially designed half-day session on how to coach their people in using the new selling and proposal writing techniques. They hoped that, by working extra hard now, they could recoup some of the improvements that would have been comparatively easy to implement earlier.

"The very best advice I can give managers," Consultant said, "is that when they've approved a training program, they should make sure the very first workshop is scheduled for *them*—and that *they attend it*." He said that nothing assures a faster, more accurate and thorough change process than managers changing first. They not only set the example, they subsequently know exactly what to look for, and how to encourage it, in the work of their subordinates. As one manager put it, "I'm glad the training department kept twisting my arm until I went to the course. I thought my writing was fine, but that a few of my people had some problems. Now *all of us* are writing better. We would have missed an opportunity for major improvement if I had stayed away as I wanted to."

"But surely," I objected, "you're not asking me to tell executives they should attend the many training programs that are run for their employees."

"Oh, you're going to tell them something even more revolutionary than that," Consultant answered. "You're going to tell them that if a course is not important enough for the boss to take, maybe nobody should have to take it."

"I am?"

"That's right. Most executive suites seem locked into the notion that the function of training—especially training in writing—is primarily remedial. That it's just a way to fix poor performance of subordinates. But they can't afford to think that way about training any more. Today the imperative for organizations to *change* is too strong. They have to start using training, deliberately and systematically, as a means of installing new, more effective ways for everyone to perform. And if we know nothing else about change, we know that it occurs in organizations from the top down. Change has to be demonstrated, not mandated."

"But let's get back to the subject of writing," he said. "I suggested the boss should attend the workshop first. But direct management involvement in any training program—especially one to improve writing—is so rare that even proposing it marks me as a dreamer. Even Plan B—getting managers to attend a two- or three-hour meeting on the writing practices and criteria to be installed—is very difficult to pull off.

"So as a realistic minimum, I propose that managers should, at the program implementation stage, do at least three things to assure the primary objectives get met. First of all, they must make sure that *every person* whose writing needs to change attends the training. Those most vociferous—or cagey—about being exempted are likely to be the most diligent later in resisting the intended improvements. Second, managers must assure that everyone *knows why* they are attending; that is, the boss should tell them, at the time he or she nominates them for training, what changes in performance will be expected.

"If managers forget, and participants don't know, what the training is intended to accomplish, people just disappear for a few days, then come back with puzzling new ideas and have to be set straight again."

Following the Intervention

"So what's the third thing executives must do?" I asked.

"After a training program, managers must monitor their people's work, encouraging them to abandon the old BoG practices and rewarding them when they use the new CleaR practices. One company, an international pharmaceutical firm, went so far as to set up a permanent senior executive committee to conduct ongoing reviews of the corporation's written communications. Both management and staff, most of whom had Ph.D.'s, were research scientists; they knew that, given their backgrounds, BoG would quickly reassert itself if the executive suite was not vigilant.

"The time immediately following training is especially critical. As I've said a hundred times, a skilled workshop leader needs two or three *days* to teach someone to write differently. In *seconds* the boss can have him writing exactly the way he did before the course. All it takes is a frown or a troubled question. 'Is *this* what they tried to teach you in that writing course?' And if the boss wants to destroy all effects of the training, he has only to declare, 'That's not the way we do it.'

"Or," Consultant added, "managers can simply ignore the improvements they see in people's writing. That takes a little longer, but it will usually eradicate the effects of training just as thoroughly—especially if the managers continue writing BoG themselves."

"You're starting to get sarcastic again," I pointed out.

"Yes, I suppose I am. But sometimes I get discouraged. You would think, after all these years. . . ."

"You know," he went on, "recently management has been learning so much about what organizations need to do to be more effective, and so much about how to manage change in order to meet new goals. If only they could see that writing is just another job that people have to start doing *differently,* and then manage the change accordingly. But they are so buffaloed by those damn Bogeys."

"Still, you said that some organizations—or at least some parts of organizations—have managed to win the Paper Wars," I ventured.

"Oh, certainly," he said.

CHAPTER 13

SOME WINNERS

*Good business writing just means
making some new choices based on
freer and more constructive criteria.*

Consultant and I sat, side by side, watching the sun disappear behind the mountains. "This has been fun," he said.

"Yes, I've enjoyed it too . . . usually."

"You mean I can be difficult to get along with?" he asked.

"One might be tempted to say that, now and again."

"Sometimes I'm crusty and opinionated. Sometimes you're cautious, sometimes even a bit dense. But I think that, between us, we managed to pull it off."

"Yes, I think so too," I said.

"I like what you did with my war stories."

"Thank you. I've been wondering, though. Most of the stories you told me were about Paper Wars defeats—or abdications, at least. Surely there have been some winners."

"Dozens," Consultant answered. "Perhaps hundreds."

"Tell me about some of them."

The Internal Auditors Start Getting the Job Done

The internal audit group of a multinational oil company was troubled that their reports weren't having much effect. Those reports contained recommendations for improving the operations of audited departments, but management seemed to ignore them.

The problem wasn't difficult to diagnose. Senior executives *never saw* the recommendations. The recommendations were always tacked onto the end of the reports, following the notations, item by item, of such discrepancies as the $19.35 that was charged to the wrong account or the 47 gallons of gasoline that couldn't be accounted for. If there were, say, 18 items discussed in the report, 3 being recommendations, the recommendations would be numbers 16, 17, and 18. They differed from the minutiae in the report only by being buried somewhere in longer paragraphs.

Therefore, the department heads and divisional managers never read past the first two or three items before setting audit reports aside for filing. They thought the reports contained nothing but the details of minor problems that had already been disposed of.

The audit manager and the two supervisors working under her were excited by Consultant's suggestion that they relegate all the minutiae to an appendix and use the report itself to state and then explain the recommendations. But when they proposed the change, the junior auditors almost revolted. Already sensitive about being about as popular as IRS representatives, they felt the new report format was dangerously confrontational.

Eventually the audit staff devoted a full half-day meeting to reaching two decisions: (1) their job was not to assure that the $19.35 was credited to the right account, but to help other departments identify and solve operational problems; and (2) presenting the audit recommendations, therefore, was the only real purpose of their reports.

"So they held their breaths and started writing their reports in the new format," Consultant said.

"What happened?" I asked.

"One of the audit supervisors called me 10 days later. He said that three senior executives had already picked up the phone to compliment the internal audit department on how useful their reports had suddenly become."

The Politicians Give the Voters CleaR

"The winning party had vowed that, if elected, it would improve communications between the provincial (i.e., state) government and the public," Consultant said. "Like most election promises, that one was soon forgotten. But it remained in effect long enough to give the public service a mandate to set up a training program in writing for government employees."

The workshops were an instant success with the people who attended and, therefore, with the people who organized them. They even produced, in the afterglow of the election, some early improvements in the documents that got written.

"Then a kind of Paper Wars stagnation set in," Consultant said. "People continued to attend the workshops, and subsequently returned to work advocating change; but managers, never having had an opportunity to buy in, continued to protect the old ways. After a few years, however, people who had taken the course earlier starting moving into middle management positions. One of the first things they often did, when taking over a department, was send everyone to the writing course. Needless to say, they also encouraged people to write better when they returned.

"Eventually, even though the politicians who had made the original promise had long since gone their separate ways, the government employees started writing correspondence that the public could read and understand. The improvement took much longer—and cost much more—than it should have. But at least it happened."

Two Giants Keep Up with the Competition

"So much needs to be changed, and so much *does* change when organizations free up their writers to start looking seriously at what readers need, that the full dimensions of most Paper Wars victories are usually difficult to document," Consultant pointed out. "But when the objective is clear-cut, success (or failure) is clear-cut as well."

He went on to tell about two famous multinationals. One we looked at earlier—the computer giant that set out to produce user manuals that, in addition to other criteria, could be used by people who read at a sixth-grade level. Having studied their readers carefully, and having taken steps to assure their manual writing practices changed to meet what they now knew about their readers, they confirmed their role as the trendsetter in the industry. Previously their documentation had been the butt of jokes, but for a time afterward it set a new standard that others had to scramble to meet.

Another giant, forced by judicial decision to start competing in a market it previously monopolized, discovered its new competitors were winning more than their share of sales because they wrote better proposals. The old spec sheet and attached price quotation just did not move equipment any more. Their decision to train 300 sales engineers how to write technical sales proposals brought an immediate payoff. One of the proposals drafted in the very first workshop produced a large sale whose profits more than paid for the entire training program.

"It's not often," Consultant said, "that an organization can so clearly put a value on a Paper Wars victory. But writing is so important to how companies and agencies operate at the day-to-day level, we know that valuable change has occurred when we see that people have started writing readable, helpful documents."

The Customers Start Getting Good Service

"Three different cases come to mind," Consultant said, "of companies that wanted to improve their customer service—but discovered they had to win a shootout with BoG first.

"One, a multinational oil company, had a relatively simple fight on its hands. The company wanted to improve its relationship with its regular customers, so it put a senior public relations executive in charge of its credit card operations. He was aghast to read the routine collection letters their computer had been sending out, especially after the initial 'perhaps you've forgotten' notice. Not only were they elaborately argued and difficult to read, many were bad-mannered and defensive. The ones that restored credit privileges after the customer had caught up with his payments were the worst of all. They only grudgingly invited him to continue as a customer and warned him sternly that he would be watched carefully in the future."

According to Consultant, the new head of credit immediately hired an outside firm to rewrite the entire series of computer letters.

* * * * *

"Then there were the *Letters of Shame*," Consultant said, laughing.

"One of our people called the president of an investment company. She explained that she was one of their clients as well as a writing consultant. She proposed that, judging from the muddled letter she'd just received, he should be talking with her about how they could modernize their customer correspondence.

"He immediately referred her to the head of their recently appointed *Letters of Shame Committee*. The committee's mandate was to find a solution to their bad writing, and she ended up conducting a series of workshops that taught their employees to write clear, positive letters to clients."

* * * * *

"You make it sound so easy," I said.

"Sometimes it can be, certainly," Consultant said. "But bad writing can also create in-depth blocks to good customer service. One of our clients decided to redefine its corporate mission. Previously it had seen itself as a company that sold natural gas and appliances—a pipeline and stove operation, in other words. Management decided, given the nature of the modern marketplace, it should now become a company that met the energy needs of its customers—that is, a people-focused operation.

"The company launched a superbly managed organizational development project, and people at all levels either joined up or were won over. But they continued to be weak at that key point, interface with the public. When customers called about problems, they still found the company service reps difficult to deal with.

"The company had a writing problem," Consultant said, "not so much a current one as an old one. The policy and procedures manuals that had accumulated over the years were impenetrable. Therefore service reps, when dealing with customers, simply didn't know what to do. They could not be sure what they were supposed to say, or what discretionary decisions they could make.

"And the manuals gave them terrible language to work with:

The customer will be required to. . . .

The Company will refuse all requests for. . . .

No one will be permitted to. . . .

Imagine the kinds of situations that arose," Consultant continued. "Imagine a young service rep, just getting the feel of her new job, picking up the phone and finding herself talking with an angry farmer. He says a heater quit and the chicks in his brooder died.

"So the service rep has to find out what to say to him. Now imagine her holding the phone under her chin while she fumbles through a stack of corporate manuals—manuals consisting of inserts that have simply accumulated over the years—trying to figure out where to start looking for the response she needs. Meanwhile the customer is waiting—and fuming.

"Then suppose, just suppose, she finds the right entry, and starts reading to the customer from the manual: 'Under no circumstances shall the Company accept responsibility for. . . .'

"And these words, angry though they may sound, at least could be understood," Consultant said. "But also imagine the plight of the rep trying to work with a customer while guided by such policy statements as:

In the event a customer requests an alteration in a billing, and, in the judgement of the Company representative, the adjusted billing should be reduced by an amount greater than that specified above, the Supervisor is to be informed. The decision will be based upon the action taken in the past when similar requests were received, and upon any special circumstances that may exist. The intent of this practice is to maintain consistency.

Consultant explained that the gas company, in order to give its reps the modern tools they needed to deal constructively with clients, created and trained a project team to perform a total overhaul of its manuals. Management first conducted a thorough review of the policies to weed out the obsolete, the unnecessary, and the confused. Then the team reorganized the manuals by job function rather than by subject matter. That is, instead of sending customer service reps to an *Operations Manual* to look for the heading "Rates," they gave them a *Customer Service Manual* that contained the heading, "Quoting Rates."

Finally, the team rewrote all the manuals so they talk about people and things rather than about concepts. When a customer service rep now turns to the section entitled "Handling Requests for a New Base Rate," he or she reads a passage which begins, "When a customer requests a new base rate, you have three options. (1) You can. . . ."

Consultant's Favorite Success Story

"Tell me your favorite story," I said. "Which organization did the best job of tackling a writing problem?"

"You may not be ready for this," he responded. "It was a small mining company in Idaho. They managed every step in the campaign like a business school case study.

"Their shift supervisors—that is, the foremen working in the mine—raised the problem initially. They complained they had a lot of writing to do, and they didn't know how to do it. Later investigation established that the shift supervisors, usually people with a high school education or less, had to write a surprising variety of short, but very important, memo-length reports. Their reports could determine whether the next shift worked productively, whether accidents occurred, whether workers were fired or promoted. The safe and profitable operation of the mine depended upon the people in head office knowing what was happening at the ore face, and the supervisors' reports provided that information.

"The company set, as its objective, helping the shift supervisors write successful reports, confidently.

"And they did an especially good job of preparing to achieve that objective, especially considering how their problem was discovered. Management's first response could well have been, 'find a writing course for the shift supervisors down at the mine.' But instead they looked at the supervisors' writing in the context of the whole operation and decided to train everyone from the CEO down. They then conducted an extensive search for a firm that could help them achieve their objective, and they insisted the workshop leader meet with every level of management before the training started.

"They carried through in the implementation stage, too. The very first workshop was attended by their senior executives, and then they methodically worked their way down through the company. By the time personnel at every level entered the training room, they knew the people above them, from the vice president down, had already been there and were committed to the practices they were about to learn. The mine supervisors were the *last* to be trained. By then everyone in the company who might read their memos was knowledgeable about writing and prepared to support them."

According to Consultant, the program finished on a gratifying note. One senior executive said, "The workshop gave us an unexpected bonus. We wanted our shift supervisors to know that they didn't have to write like geologists and engineers. By the time we all took the course, the rest of us—including our geologists and engineers—had learned the same thing."

Winning Is Not Only Easy, It Feels Better

Consultant went on for some time that evening, but I don't think I should. His war stories all make the same point. When management decides it wants better writing, and when it decides to make sure it gets better writing, writing improves. But as long as management remains ambivalent or uncommitted, the Paper Wars continue, and the organization's written communications fail to do the job they are supposed to do.

After Consultant left, I sat in the dark thinking. Too many executives indeed seem to be afraid to let their people write well. Thanks to the Bogeys, they seem more afraid of the bad things that *might* happen if they promote CleaR than of the bad things that *do* happen because they protect BoG.

Because of their own discomforts and uncertainties, executives avoid getting involved in managing writing constructively. Either they try to ignore the problem, or they continue to apply nonsolutions that, though they don't work, at least minimize management's risk.

As to Consultant's assertion that learning to write well is comparatively easy, I was dubious in the beginning. But now, having heard him out, I'm beginning to understand what he means. Although we live in a literate society surrounded by public writing that is, for the most part, clear and purposeful, many people spend several hours each day encapsulated in a working environment where an aberrant form—BoG—has evolved as the prevailing, supposedly appropriate standard. Yet BoG is nothing more than a narrow slice of the techniques a writer can use. Moreover, each BoG technique is the *least* communicative, from a reader's point of view, of the various alternatives a writer might choose. The purveyors of BoG, motivated by their fears of the written word, have chosen to cast their lot with the practices that put the greatest distance between the writer and the reader, the most words between reader and understanding. As Consultant says, nobody wants to read BoG. They only want to write it.

People are hesitant to imitate outside models. They seem to think those who work for organizations write under special constraints. Yet business and government writing, in comparison to more general writing, is easier, not more difficult, because it is thoroughly functional. Other writers have to catch and hold an audience. But organizational writers start with captive readers, and they have only to convince those readers of *what needs to be done,* or *explain how.* Therefore the range of competencies needed to write effectively in business and government is relatively narrow and quite manageable by people without special writing talents. What is difficult for many people to overcome is the feeling that words, once written down, acquire a magnified power to offend.

So as Consultant points out, good business writing is "easy" in that it just means making some new choices based on freer and more constructive criteria. If we listen, our Reader Within can provide us with excellent guidance as to what those criteria should be and how to apply them. The writing practices that result in CleaR are easier to learn— and easier to use—than those that result in BoG. The *only* thing to be said against them is that, initially at least, they are likely to stir up the Change Stoppers of people accustomed to writing BoG.

Writing will always be hard work. But when the individual, and the organization, learns to use writing as a constructive way of helping others do their jobs—as a form of cooperative effort that contributes to achieving the mutual goals of the sender and the receiver—writing can become rewarding work as well. Success always feels better than continued failure, no matter how safe failure may pretend to be.

INDEX

ABOUT THE AUTHOR

Don M. Ricks is the former CEO and current Director for Research and Development for IWCC Training in Writing Ltd., a world-wide training firm with headquarters in Toronto, Ontario. Every week dozens of people across North America attend writing workshops he designed.

He has worked as a professional writing consultant to many leading international corporations, including IBM, AT&T, and Westinghouse Electronics and Defense, for over 20 years. After earning a football letter, Phi Beta Kappa key, and B.A. in English at the University of Wyoming, he spent a Fulbright year at Bristol University in England. Then he received an M.A. from Northwestern University as a Woodrow Wilson Fellow and a Ph.D in English from the University of Missouri in 1965. After a short successful career in academia, he turned to consulting.

For more information about the firm, write or call IWCC Training in Writing Ltd., Suite 209, 30 East Beaver Creek Road, Richmond Hill, Ontario, Canada L4B 1J2 (telephone 416 764-3710).